To Janet John

TIPS FROM THE GARDEN HOTLINE

Tips from
the Garden Hotline
Ralph Snodsmith

TAYLOR PUBLISHING COMPANY
Dallas, Texas

Illustrations by Harvey Shirai
with assistance by Jay Cotton

Copyright © 1984 by Ralph L. Snodsmith

Published by Taylor Publishing Company
1550 West Mockingbird Lane, Dallas, Texas 75235

Library of Congress Cataloging in Publication Data

Snodsmith, Ralph, 1939-
  Tips from the garden hotline.

  1. Gardening — Miscellanea. I. Title.
SB453.S595   1984   635   84-1
ISBN 0-87833-380-0

Printed in the United States of America

*Dedicated to
the friends of the "Garden Hotline"*

CONTENTS

INDOORS

OUTDOORS

VEGETABLES

GENERAL HORTICULTURE

PESTS

INTRODUCTION

In response to the pleas of many devoted listeners of the Garden Hotline, as well as former students and my many gardening friends, I have assembled some of their most frequently asked questions and have tried to discuss the most common answer to each problem. These answers are all in a non-technical form which, I believe, will help even a novice gardener.

I have found that using humor and catch-phrases helps people to remember the answers that evolve out of a discussion or lecture. That is why, along with the humorous illustrations which accompany each subject, you will discover that I have described certain subjects using such non-technical terminology as: "wet feet" — the roots of plants standing in a water-saturated soil; "egg water" — a source of nutrition for some plants; "black gold" — a valuable source of organic matter; "cotton balls" — a clue to insect identification; and "you be the bee" — a technique for artificial pollination. "Rusty nails," "underground railroad," and "roots and shoots" are other examples of catch-phrases I have used over the years in my discussions of questions from both indoor and outdoor gardeners.

Gardening problems are universal. Over 44 million American households are involved with gardening in one fashion or another, and all of them have problems from time to time. You are not alone when you wonder why your spider plant has not produced babies, or what new "critter" is attacking your gardenia plant, or why your cucurbits have completely collapsed.

As you read this book, I would like you to *enjoy* learning something about gardening. But, most of all, I would like you to *enjoy* taking proper care of your plants so you can "just step back and watch them grow!"

INDOORS

HOUSEPLANTS
Water: The #1 Killer

It is a known fact that over-watering is the number one killer of houseplants. For some reason, any time a plant starts to drop leaves, wilt, or show signs of yellowing, we run and get the watering can. Don't! Water needs are determined by many conditions: the type of plant, temperature, humidity, soil type, light, and time of year are just a few factors that determine water requirements. Some plants like it dry and some must be kept slightly moist. During hot weather the transpiration rate is increased and a plant may need more water to keep it cool. Humidity levels also influence water requirements. During humid periods soil will dry more slowly and the plant will transpire less. Soils vary greatly in ability to hold moisture. Newer, artificial soil mixes tend to hold more water than standard potting soils.

The amount of light the plant receives will also increase or decrease its need for water. In high light conditions, a plant generally requires more water for cooling and food manufacturing. The season is important, because some plants go into a dormant state for a period of time during which they require less water. During active growth they will definitely need more water

When is the best time to water a plant? Some say in the morning, and some say in the afternoon or evening. I say, "When it needs it." Don't fall into the trap of watering (whether it needs it or not) every Friday afternoon. You may have some plants in your collection that need water once a month and some that need it daily.

How much water to give is another question. The "tea cup" method is not the best for most plants. In general, give them a big drink when needed and then allow them to dry some between waterings. There are exceptions to this rule, of course. Coleus, begonias, impatiens, and Wandering Jew are just a few that must be kept moist at all times.

Exceptions in the other direction are: cactus, jade, ponytail palm, Christmas cactus, as well as many others. Let these plants dry considerably between waterings. Learn the individual requirements of all your plants. Don't be guilty of overwatering.

POTS, POTS, AND MORE POTS
For Happy Houseplants

A walk through any garden center will show you the many types of pots that are available for houseplants. These include clay, plastic, ceramic, metal, fiberglass, etc. Which one is best for your plants? By learning about the advantages and disadvantages of each type you can make your own decision.

Start with clay pots. They have been with us almost since the beginning of time. They come in many sizes, from the tiny thimble pots to the giant terra-cotta planters. They have one drainage hole in the bottom and come in one color. The greatest advantage of the clay pot is that it breathes — air and moisture actually pass through the sides of the pot. This allows the soil to dry evenly and not pull away from the inside of the pot, making the watering practice easier. However, clay pots are heavy and tend to accumulate algae and moss growth on their sides.

Plastic pots are lightweight, come in many colors, and have four holes in the bottom for improved drainage. They do not breathe. When the soil begins to dry it pulls away from the sides, making it necessary to adjust the watering practices. When watering a plant that has been allowed to dry considerably, water will quickly run out the bottom holes. The natural assumption would be that the plant has plenty of water. This is not true. The water flows around the edges so that the soil inside is still dry. Water must be allowed to resoak the entire soil ball.

Ceramic, metal, and fiberglass containers often have no hole in the bottom. This spells disaster from the start. Water can collect in the bottom, causing root rot. Watering practices must be adjusted. The best way to use a container with no drainage hole is to double pot. This simply means growing the plant in a clay pot set inside the decorative, drainless container. A ring of algae may form on the bottom of the clay pot, creating a seal and plugging up drainage. To alleviate this problem, place a layer of sand in the bottom of the drainless container, so the clay pot does not make contact with it. Double potting makes just about any container a useful planter.

POTTING MIXES
Whip Up Your Own

Potting mixes are made up of varying amounts of different components. No two brands will be alike. They may contain potting soil, peat moss, vermiculite, perlite, or sand. Each ingredient has a function in the mix.

Soils used in potting mixes are generally high in organic content that holds nutrients so critical to plant growth. A potting soil that is taken from one part of the country will be different from the soil taken from another area.

Soil is made up of sand, silt, and clay particles, with humic acid as the cement that holds them together (as well as apart). Humic acid is the end product of decaying organic matter, and it is what gives the soil its color.

Peat moss is added to increase moisture-holding capacity, to hold nutrients, and to provide bulk.

Vermiculite (which can hold hundreds of times its own weight in water) is also used to increase moisture-holding capacity. It is often used in mixes for plants that do not like to dry out between waterings. If you have a tendency to over-water your plants do not use vermiculite.

Perlite is used to provide bulk and aeration, and to improve drainage. It helps loosen the mix and makes it lighter in weight. Because of its light weight, perlite is great for hanging baskets, in place of other drainage materials such as sand. Sand is often added to the mix to provide weight and improve drainage.

To make a soil mix you must know the water requirements of the plant. If the plant likes extremely well-drained soil, the soil mix can be adjusted accordingly. The standard mix that I make is one part potting soil, one part sand or perlite, and one part peat moss. Combine these thoroughly and you will have a suitable mix for most of your plants. If better drainage is needed, add two parts perlite or sand. You will probably need to water more often, but you won't over-water.

HOUSEPLANT LIGHTING
Paying the Energy Bill

Plants can be grown in just about any area if they receive light. As a matter of fact, you do not need a sunny window or any window at all. Artificial light will generally allow plants to grow and flourish if given in sufficient quality and quantity. In most homes there are combinations of two types of artificial light, incandescent and fluorescent.

Incandescent lights are the regular type of light bulbs, but they are too hot for a plant if placed close enough to provide adequate light for growth. The heat generated by incandescent bulbs can cook the growing tips and foliage of the plants. There are incandescent plant lights that are designed to alleviate this problem, if used properly. They come in several different wattages that give off different amounts of light.

Fluorescent lights are more efficient because they use less energy. They generate little heat and can be placed close to the plant, which can then benefit from the increased exposure to the light. Several different types of fluorescent lights have been developed as plant lights. They will provide the needed spectrum of light not only for growth, but for flowering too. A combination of a cool-white and a warm-white fluorescent will provide adequate light for most plants. In some cases both fluorescent and incandescent lights are used in combination. The amount of time the lights should be on depends on the plants requirements. If you don't want to pay high electric bills, grow plants that require low light.

LIGHT FOR HOUSEPLANTS
It's Free!

Not everyone can afford the electric bill that it takes to provide artificial light to make plants grow. That's okay, because we can take advantage of the natural light that comes through the windows of our homes or apartments. Of course, the light differs depending on the direction the window faces. Also, obstructions in front of the window, such as trees and buildings, can alter the amount of light received.

Light quality and quantity also differ depending on the time of year. During the winter a north window may receive very little light, but during the summer the amount of light will be greatly increased. The south window has a different problem. During the winter the sun, being lower in the sky, provides great quantities of light for the south window. During the summer, with the sun high in the sky, less light is received. A caution on the south window: during the winter the heat build-up can be tremendous and the plants can cook. For windows of east or west exposure, the quality and quantity of light are basically the same throughout the year. The only difference is that afternoon light received through the west window is generally warmer than morning light received through the east window.

As the seasons change, inventory the amount of light your plants are receiving. It may be necessary to move the plants to a brighter or darker window depending on their needs.

Light received through any particular window is classified using three terms: *full sun,* the direct exposure of the plant to sun for the entire day; *partial sun,* one half day or less of direct sun; and *filtered light,* no direct sun at all (this could be anywhere to the side of the window). Of course, the farther away you place the plant from the source of light the more moderate the light becomes. Pick the best light for your plants. Find out how much light they need, and use common sense.

HUMIDITY FOR HOUSEPLANTS
The Sahara Desert?

Misting is great for you, psychologically, but it does very little for most of your plants. Mist a plant and put the mister away. Come back and look at the foliage. The leaves are already dry. You have only temporarily increased the moisture around your plant. If you could mist at least fifty times a day it might help. A plant is better off if you increase the humidity on a permanent basis.

During the winter, the air in most of our homes becomes as dry as the Sahara Desert — 5% humidity or less. More moisture in the air will not only benefit your plants — it will enable you to turn down the thermostat and conserve energy since you will feel comfortable at a lower temperature when the humidity is in the acceptable range of 45%-55%.

To increase humidity on a more permanent basis than misting, you can run a humidifier, make humidity trays, and/or grow hundreds of houseplants.

Humidifiers come in many styles and sizes. If you decide this is the best method for you, be sure you follow the manufacturer's directions on keeping it clean, because certain fungus problems can be transmitted into the air.

Humidity trays are nothing more than deep, water-tight trays. Place a layer of sand or gravel in the bottom of the tray. Add water and place your plant on top of the sand or gravel — not in the water. A plant sitting directly above the tray of water will be helped by the moisture as it evaporates and thus increases the humidity. You will need to add water to the tray on a regular basis.

Growing hundreds of houseplants will also add humidity. Evaporation from the soil, and the water given off by the foliage, will constantly add moisture to the air in the home.

Try a combination of these methods to increase the humidity — but, in general, forget the misting.

FERTILIZING HOUSEPLANTS
Feed Me!

Every plant shop you visit has a multitude of houseplant fertilizers. Some are for all plants, some are for foliage plants, and some are for specific plants, such as African violets, bromeliads, cactus, etc. Which one should you use? First of all, *read the label.* The manufacturer has spent thousands of dollars figuring out how his product works best. It is probably true that if you follow the directions on the label, under normal circumstances your plant will grow.

If you understand what is in the fertilizer and what your plant needs, you can choose the best formula. Generally, houseplant nutrients include nitrogen, phosphorus, and potassium (N-P-K). The percentages of each nutrient always are found on the label in that order: for example, 15-30-15. The first number, 15, is the percent of nitrogen; the second number, 30, is the percent of phosphorus; and the third number, 15, is the potassium.

My philosophy for feeding houseplants is to use a low nitrogen in relation to the phosphorus for flowering plants: for example, 5-10-10. Phosphorus stimulates flowering, so the first number on the label should he smaller than the second number. For foliage plants use a fertilizer with the first number higher than the second: for example, 12-6-6. Nitrogen stimulates better foliage. There are so many brands on the market today that I could fill several pages just with numbers.

Some important nutrients that are often overlooked are the trace, or minor, elements. These are nutrients that must be present in the soil in minute quantities. Examples might be boron, magnesium, sulfur, etc. If they are present in the fertilizer they will be listed on the label. Remember, a plant growing in a pot has no way to secure additional nutrients unless you supply them.

How often should you feed your plants? It depends on the type of fertilizer you use. Some are added to every watering and some as infrequently as every six months. You must follow the directions on the label for best results. In general, I feed my houseplants regularly on a 12-month schedule. As long as my plants are growing, they need nutrients.

"Brrrrrr! Who turned down the heat?"

HOUSEPLANTS
The Energy Crisis

During the 70's there was one international crisis that had a pronounced beneficial effect on our houseplants — the energy crisis. Because of it, we needed to conserve energy, and, among other efforts, we turned down our thermostats. Our houseplants enjoyed every bit of it, and began to produce stronger stems, larger leaves, and even to set better blossoms.

When the temperature is reduced it takes less moisture to raise the humidity. With the plant giving off less water to dry air, moisture is used as part of the plant's building blocks, giving rise to larger leaves. Plants that are cool do not grow as fast, but they develop stronger stems with shorter internodes. The space between the leaves is reduced, creating stockier, fatter, fuller plants. The daytime temperature is somewhat difficult to control, but can be influenced by shading or blocking out light.

A lower night temperature is very important for proper plant growth, because plants that are too warm at night often become extremely leggy. If a differential of at least 10 degrees is maintained between day and night temperatures, most plants will benefit. During cool nights less energy is required by the plant. By turning down the thermostat at night, we can influence the growth of most of our plants in a positive manner, and save money, too.

Of course there are always exceptions to every rule, and the African violet is our example this time. It likes to be warm at night.

HOUSEPLANTS
Light Up My Leaves

As the schefflera and weeping fig develop new growth at the top, often the inner, older leaves at the bottom begin to fall. This is the natural result of the fact that light is not reaching the inner foliage. Mother Nature is telling the plant to drop leaves that are no longer needed. To reduce the loss of inner foliage, artificial light can be applied. The right amount of light fools Mother Nature and these leaves will not be discarded.

Lighting of the inner foliage is quite simple. Use a small, globe-type lamp with a 60-watt incandescent bulb. Place it on the floor so the light shines up through the plant. Turn the light on for 12 to 14 hours daily. Provide adequate protection from pets and children, because the light fixture may be hot. Also, arrange the cord so no one trips over it.

Heat will dry out the growth tips of the plant. So, in positioning the light, check the heat generated from the light bulb by holding your hand next to the leaf closest to the light. If the back of your hand feels warm, move the light further away.

Aesthetically a pleasing by-product of bottom lighting is the effect of the shadows cast on the wall.

"I hope that egg water is for me."

CALCIUM
Egg Water??

Remember all those times your mother reminded you to "drink your milk so you'll grow up to be strong and healthy?" She was right. Calcium is important in our diets to build strong bones and healthy teeth, and it is important for the growth of our plants, too. It builds strong stems and roots, and can help release nutrients from the soil for use by the plant.

Calcium is added to the soil in the form of lime. For those plants that like only slightly acid or more alkaline soil, lime is beneficial. African violets love it. In fact, in their natural habitat, they are often found on limestone cliffs.

If you don't feel like lugging home a 50-pound bag of lime, you can go to your kitchen for a substitute. Egg water and eggshells are a great source of calcium for plants. However, if you are using water in which you have boiled eggs, cool it before you pour it on your plants. Otherwise you will scald them.

Eggshells can be crushed and sprinkled on the surface of the soil, or combined in the potting mix. If you use shells, be sure to remove the membranous lining, or when it begins to decay, you will think someone forgot to take out the garbage. Eggshells can be soaked in water in order to leach out the calcium. The same rule applies about removing the membranous tissue first.

Eggs are great for you, and for your plants.

IRON: A MINOR ELEMENT
A Rusty Nail

Iron is necessary in the development of chlorophyll, the green in the plant. Chlorosis (a yellowing of the leaves) in plants can be due to a lack of sufficient iron. This chlorotic condition often shows in the newest growth first. The veins of the leaves may be darker than the tissue between the veins. Two plants that often suffer from iron chlorosis are the gardenia and the citrus. Both need iron to develop properly. Both plants like an acid soil for good growth.

Since plants have the ability to absorb iron through their leaves, one way to supply iron is through foliar application. Chelated iron solution, available commercially, can be used as a soil drench, as well as for foliar application.

The rusty, old, washed-out steel wool pad that is lying on the kitchen counter can supply great quantities of iron also. Crumble the pad over the soil and, in time, the iron will become available to the plant. Rusty nails can also be pushed into the soil to insure a long-term supply of iron.

Caution on the use of iron: if too much is applied, the leaves can show signs of burn and turn so deep green in color you will think they are black. This is a case of "if one ounce will do it, two will not do it better."

If iron chlorosis is suspected, apply chelated iron and positive results should be observed within a few days. If improvement does not occur, consider other causes of chlorosis such as poor drainage, a cold environment, exposure to too much sunlight, or poor nutrition. Your local Cooperative Extension agent or garden center operator can help you decide.

STERILIZED POTTING SOIL
Cook Your Own

Potting soil that has been sterilized to help control insects and weeds is available at the garden center. However, little can be done to sterilize soils for diseases without killing desirable bacteria and destroying the structure of the soil itself.

If you wish to sterilize your own potting soil there is an easy way to do it right in the kitchen. If regular garden soil is to be one of the ingredients in your soil mix, you can sterilize it against insects and weeds by baking it in the oven.

Moisten the soil to be sterilized so that when it is squeezed in the hand, and pressure is released, a firm ball of earth remains. (If water runs out between the fingers, it is too moist, and when cooked, it will come out as a brick.) On a large cookie sheet, make a big "meatloaf" of the moistened soil. Insert a meat thermometer. Place your mix in the oven and turn the temperature to 225 degrees. When the thermometer reads 180 degrees turn the oven down to 180 degrees and let the soil cook for at least 30 minutes. The soil will then be sterilized. Before using the soil, be sure to let it cool.

A strange odor may be emitted during the cooking process. That is ammonia being released by the bacteria in the soil and it is harmless. Just open the window and air out the kitchen.

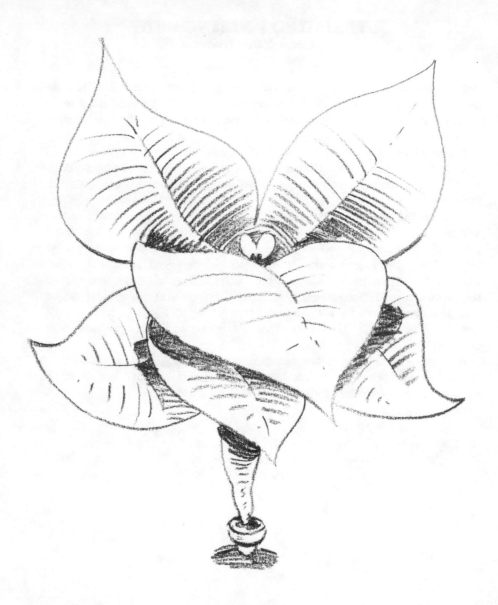

"I think it's time to move to bigger quarters."

REPOTTING HOUSEPLANTS
To Move, or Not to Move?

Plants can stay in the same container for years if they are maintained with proper nutrition and if the soil is alive with desirable bacteria. However, if a plant is not fed properly, the root system will eventually search out and use up all the nutrients. The plant will stop growing and possibly begin to decline in health.

When is it time to repot a plant? If the sides of the pot are beginning to break, it's time. The only other way to tell is to slip the plant out of the container and examine the roots. Water the plant thoroughly first. This will protect the roots, and it is easier to handle moist soil. If the plant is too large to be handled by one person, call in a friend.

Slip the plant out of the pot. If some of the roots are in a coil at the bottom, it does not mean that the plant needs repotting. Just cut the coil off, put fresh potting soil in the bottom of the pot to fill the void where the coiled roots were removed, and then replace the plant. But if the sides of the soil ball are a total mass of roots, then think of repotting.

If repotting is necessary use the same type of soil that the plant is presently growing in. If a sandy mix was used, use a sandy mix again, etc. The plant may not like it if you change the type of mix.

For example: If a plant is growing in a peat mix, and is transplanted into a sandy mix, without removing all of the peat mix, two different moisture-holding conditions will exist. When the plant is watered, water will run through the sandy mix and it will dry much faster than the peat mix. The roots that grow in the sandy section may dehydrate and those growing in the peat may rot. Without a healthy root system the plant may die.

Most of our houseplants love to be somewhat potbound so don't be in a hurry to repot.

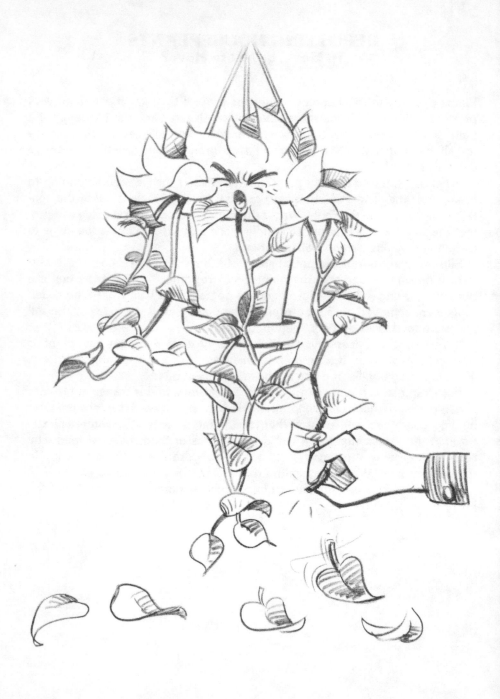

PINCHING PLANTS
Ouch!

"Pinching" a plant hurts you more than it does the plant. In fact, if the plant could, it would give a sigh of relief. Pinching removes the growing tip and activates several stimuli in the plant which encourage development of side branches, keep the plant full and compact, and affect flowering.

Using the thumb and index finger, snap out the growing tip and you have pinched the plant. If this is performed on the newest growth, it is called a "soft pinch"; and when performed on the older growth, further back on the stem, it is known as a "hard pinch." This may have to be done with a pruning tool.

Many plants in hanging baskets need regular pinching or they will end up with all the desirable foliage growing near the floor. Regular pinching of hanging plants encourages inner growth development, keeping them fat and full.

For specimen plants, such as the large-leafed rubber plant, pinching encourages branching. Otherwise the plant will look like a "telephone pole" with just a few leaves at the top.

In the garden, pinching is done not only to provide a bushy plant but also to direct energy to plant parts, such as the flowers. To make a single larger flower, the side buds are pinched out. This is called "disbudding."

Pinching also encourages more flowers on plants that bloom on new growth. *Columnea* can be kept blooming continually by immediately pinching the tips of the branches which have spent blossoms. This pinch causes the plant to produce new growth.

CLEANING HOUSEPLANTS
Give 'em a Bath

"What's the ficus doing in the shower?" (That's right, in the shower.) This could be a question in my home. Of course the plant did not walk into the shower by itself. I put it there. Why? To keep it clean.

One of the best ways to keep most houseplants clean is to give them a bath. This can be done in the kitchen sink, in the bathtub, or in the shower. Houseplants such as ficus, philodendron, pothos, ivy, palms, and others with shiny foliage tend to collect dirt and dust as they grow in the home. The best way to remove the dust is to rinse the foliage with running water. Don't use soap or detergent, or a rough cloth to wipe the leaves. That would remove the cuticle layer which gives the plant its natural shine, and with the cuticle layer gone the leaves would have a dull, lackluster look. You could use the commercial sprays which are available, but they become dust catchers too. Just rinse the foliage with lukewarm water — not steaming hot or icy cold, just lukewarm.

There are plants that *cannot* take a shower. They include those with pubescence (tiny little hairs) on their leaves. African violets and purple passion plants are good examples. To clean these plants use a sable brush, the kind artists use when they paint with watercolors. Dust the leaves with the soft brush to remove the dirt and dust. Some horticulturists have suggested rinsing the foliage with slightly warm water, and then drying the leaves by shaking them gently. I have not had success with this method. The leaves often spot and begin to decay.

ROTATING HOUSEPLANTS
The Leaning Tower of Pisa?

Houseplants that are growing near a bright light will begin to grow in the direction of that light. This is called photokinesis: the reaching for light. Notice the trees and shrubs at the edge of a forest. They look as if they were growing at an angle, because they are reaching toward the light.

Indoors, you can eliminate the leaning-tower-of-Pisa look by rotating the plant 180 degrees each time it is watered. This will provide balanced light on all sides and keep the plant growing in an upright position. Outdoors, there is little that can be done, short of removing all adjacent plants.

If you doubt that plants can reach for light, the next time you start new seedlings, place them in a bright, sunny east or west window. By the end of the day they will be leaning toward the light source. The next morning, turn the plants so they face the dark side of the room. By evening the plants will have turned completely toward the light. They did it all on their own.

VACATION WATERING I
The Bathtub

Have you ever asked friends to water your houseplants while you were away on vacation, only to return to a real mess? You told them to water each Friday, but when Friday arrived they decided to play golf. ("I will water them Saturday.") When Saturday came they didn't have time, because they had to go shopping. They decided they would give your plants twice as much water on Sunday to make up for it — and they did. This could be the beginning of the end.

There are several alternatives to trusting a friend, one of which is the bathtub. This works for plants that are in clay pots. Line the bottom of the tub with paper to prevent the enamel finish from being scratched. Place regular building bricks (red clay) on top of the paper. Close the drain or put the stopper in. Then set the clay pots on top of the clay bricks and add water up to the top edge of the bricks — no deeper. You do not want the pots standing in water. The clay bricks and the clay pots will act as a siphon, keeping the soil slightly moist at all times.

After placing the plants in the tub turn the light switch on to provide constant light while you are gone. Tape the switch in the "on" position and close the door to trap the humidity in the bathroom. Give your neighbors the key and ask them to add water to the tub if needed. (The reason for taping the light switch in the "on" position: you can always trust your friends to turn out the lights, and you don't want that.)

This system will work for weeks, as long as there is water in the tub. You may even find that your plants are in better shape than when you left them.

Have a nice trip.

VACATION WATERING II
Don't Trust a Friend

Going away? Do you trust a friend to water your plants while you are away? By planning ahead, you can provide enough water for those plants even if you are gone two to three weeks, *without* trusting a friend. However, all systems recommended here must be tried in advance to make sure they work properly for you.

Give a plant a big drink of water and let it drain thoroughly. Then wrap the pot with plastic wrap. Allow the wrap to extend enough above the pot so it can be folded over to touch the stem. This will stop evaporation from the soil and keep the moisture available for the plant.

The clear plastic bag is another plant-sitter. Again, water the plant properly. Then place it, the pot and all, in the bag. Blow up the bag or support it so it does not touch the foliage of the plant. Seal it tightly, and you're ready to go away. You have just created a greenhouse or terrarium effect.

The plant will become used to high humidity and if removed immediately from this protected environment, without gradual acclimatization, leaf drop and browning of foliage tips may occur. When you return and are ready to remove the plant, make a few slits in the side of the bag to gradually lower the humidity around the plant.

For a plant that enjoys constant moisture, such as an African violet, a coleus, or a fibrous rooted begonia, the wick system will do; but it must be installed when you pot the plant, by inserting a fiber wick through the hole in the bottom of the pot. Make sure one end is shredded out into the soil and the other end is suspended into a reservoir of water. This watering method takes care of a plant by keeping the soil constantly moist, as long as the water supply is maintained.

Remember, try all of these systems *before* going away.

VACATION WATERING III
Drip, Drip, Drip

Large specimen plants, such as schefflera, ficus, palms, and dracaenas, can be watered for extended periods of time with a drip system. It is similar to the old Chinese torture — drip, drip, drip. The secret lies in the number of drips and the frequency of their occurrence.

Clean a cottage cheese or plastic deli container. Thread a small needle with the largest thread possible. Push the needle down through the bottom of the container and pull enough thread through to allow several inches to hang below the container. Tie a knot in the end of the thread that remains inside the container. Pull the knot tight against the inside bottom. To test this, fill the container with water and place it over a measuring cup. If it drips approximately a quarter cup of water in a 24-hour period, it is ready to be placed on the surface of the soil of the big plant. If it drips more than that, tie a larger knot in the thread and pull the knot tighter against the inside bottom of the container. This will help plug the hole. Remeasure the drips. The number of containers needed to water the plant depends totally on the size of the pot and the moisture requirements of the plant. A two-pound cottage cheese container will last a long time.

If you need to be away for a *long* period of time, you can ask friends to refill the container, but don't let them water the plant.

PROPAGATION
The Cheapest Little Greenhouse

What is the cheapest little greenhouse in the world? Why, it's the clear plastic bag. It can be used to propagate plants both for indoors and outdoors. It allows light to enter, and it provides a humid environment.

Take coarse builders' sand or other propagation mix, moisten it, and place three to four inches of the medium into the bag. Testing for moisture content is simple. Tip the bag onto its side and hold it in that position for one minute. If water collects in the corner of the bag, the medium is too wet. Do *not* poke a hole in the bag to let the water out. Just add more dry mix.

Cuttings can be taken from many plants and rooted. Dust the base of the cuttings with a rooting hormone and push it into the medium in the bag. Insert props or blow up the bag so the leaves do not touch the plastic, as water will collect at that point of contact and rot will result.

How can you tell if a cutting is rooted? Simple. Open up the bag and pull up a cutting (gently). If the cutting has roots, pot it up. If there are no roots, put it back and seal the bag. Be patient a little longer.

A tip on rooting hormone: some labels indicate you can dip the cutting right into the hormone container. I don't recommend that. Place a small quantity of the hormone on a piece of paper and roll the base of the cuttings in it. Discard the leftover hormone that's on the paper; don't put it back in the container. If you dip a cutting into the container, and the cutting has any disease, there is a potential of inoculating the entire supply of hormone.

PROPAGATION
A Bigger Cheap Little Greenhouse

When the "baggie" system does not make a big enough propagation unit, look in the closet. You probably have the makings of a larger greenhouse: a dry-cleaning bag. Be sure to choose the clear plastic kind that does not have holes in it. Clear plastic allows light to penetrate. Colored plastic, such as the blue or green type, will block out the light needed for plants to grow. Holes in the bag will let out the needed moisture and the plants will dry out and die.

Straighten three wire coat hangers. Then, bend them into "U"-shaped wickets. Find an old wooden box with sides about three to five inches high. Place the points of the hangers inside, and anchor the ends with bent nails or staples. Fill the box with moist propagation mix. Place cuttings that have been treated with rooting hormone into the media. Slip the box, with the hanger loops, into the plastic dry-cleaning bag and seal both ends. It will look like a covered wagon, but you will have a fantastic propagation chamber, or homemade greenhouse.

There should be no need to add water until the cuttings have rooted. By then the cuttings are ready to pot up or plant outside. This is a unit that will hold up to one hundred ivy cuttings, one hundred azalea cuttings, or fifty geranium cuttings. You are now a greenhouse operator!

"I'll be back for the final operation later."

AIR LAYERING HOUSEPLANTS
A Bandage

When the dieffenbachias, dracaenas, or scheffleras grow so tall that they reach the ceiling, there are only two things to do. A carpenter can be called to raise the roof, or air layering can be performed.

Air layering will be a conversation piece, because of the "bandage" that is used in the process. Measure down 18 to 24 inches from the top of the plant. Use a sharp knife to make three evenly spaced, 1½-inch longitudinal slits, around the main stem. These up-and-down slits should be deep enough to penetrate the bark and just enter the woody tissue — no deeper. Do not cut through to the other side! Push wooden match sticks into the wounds and break off the matches so they won't interfere with the rest of the process. These wedges will help hold the wounds open and keep them from healing too fast, as it is from these incisions that roots will originate. Dust the wounded areas with a rooting hormone powder. Then moisten sphagnum moss and pack it around the wounds. Wrap the moss with clear plastic and tie the plastic at the top and bottom. You now have the bandage. Periodically, without opening the plastic, examine it to see if droplets of water are visible on the inside of the plastic, indicating that the moss is moist. If condensation is not present loosen the top tie and add more water. At the same time check for the emergence of the new roots, which will appear as white hairs on the inside of the plastic. The whole rooting procedure may take as long as eight to ten weeks, so be patient.

After roots are observed, again using a sharp knife, cut off the top of the plant just below the bandage area. Remove the plastic, but don't try to pull off any of the moss. You will break the roots if you do. Pot this new plant in a proper mix and now you have saved the cost of a carpenter.

DIVIDING HOUSEPLANTS
With an Ax?

There is a plant family commonly grown in the home that really enjoys be-ing divided. They are the ferns. As a potted plant, a fern becomes extreme-ly rootbound and overly crowded in a short period of time. When the plant becomes crowded, it begins to die out in the center, and the roots become so dense that the plant actually begins to jack itself out of the pot. Instead of throwing it out, divide it.

Water the plant thoroughly before removing it from the pot. It is not good to handle plants with dry roots. Then using a strong butcher knife, cut the massive ball into four sections. This can be a grueling task. You may feel more like using an ax to chop them apart! When you are finished dividing, however, you will have four new plants.

A remedy for the dying out of the center of the fern is to make an "angel food cake" by cutting out the center of the fern with a strong, thin-bladed knife. Refill the hole, where you removed the core, with a well-drained mix, and water the plant. In no time at all the center will be rejuvenated with tender new shoots.

Some favorite ferns for the home include: the Boston fern, button fern, and ribbon fern. They all need filtered light, and must be kept slightly moist at all times. High humidity is essential. Also, ferns are big eaters. Feed them with a high-nitrogen plant food, such as 8-7-6 or its equivalent.

BUYING THAT SPECIMEN HOUSEPLANT
Trauma Treatment

Whether you are purchasing a six-foot *Ficus benjamina,* a seven-foot false aralia, or an eight-foot palm, I can guarantee the plant will go into shock the moment it is brought home. This will happen no matter how careful you are, even when you buy from a reputable grower. I do not recommend a purchase from a cut-rate, roadside peddler. You have no one to turn to if the plant doesn't grow.

Almost immediately the plant will begin to drop leaves. This may even happen although the leaves remain totally green. This is Mother Nature's method of conserving energy and getting the plant adjusted to the new environment. The plant was probably grown in a tropical greenhouse with extra-high humidity. When it is taken to a new environment with a much lower humidity, it sends a signal throughout its system yelling, "Conserve moisture!" — so the plant drops some leaves. The natural human reaction is to run for the watering can to give it a big drink, which is the wrong thing to do.

Several steps can be taken to alleviate excessive leaf drop. One is to purchase specimen plants during the late spring and summer when the humidity is highest in our homes. This will allow the maximum time for the plant to adjust before the heating season returns the home to a low-humidity condition.

Another method used to help plants adjust is to remove up to 50% of the foliage by hand. Simply pick off leaves here and there, thereby reducing the plant's need for water. I know this will kill *you,* but not the plant. Do it immediately.

Finally, make a tent out of a clear plastic dry-cleaning bag and place the plant inside it. You may be able to trick the plant into thinking it is back in the greenhouse. Then, after a week or so, make a few slits in the bag to allow for the exchange of dry and humid air. Make a few more slits every two days until your plant gradually adjusts to its new environment.

Throughout, you should follow the watering practices advised by your garden center operator.

HANGING BASKETS
Foliage

Foliage hanging baskets, grown primarily for their foliage chracteristics rather than for flowers, can add life to the home environment and can even be used as drapery for the window. Unique growth habits and leaf colors can be quite interesting, since not all are just green. In general, most foliage hanging baskets require filtered bright light and a high-nitrogen plant food, such as 12-6-6 or its equivalent. Watering requirements vary considerably.

I have two favorites which display lush green foliage, as well as color. They are *Epipremnum* (pothos) and *Plectranthus* (Swedish ivy).

There are two major varieties of pothos: the standard combination of green and cream or yellow leaves, and the newer variety "Marble Queen" with green and a nearly pure-white foliage. The soil of both should be allowed to become dry to the touch between waterings; they cannot stand "wet feet." Pinching pothos regularly encourages branching near the base of the stems and helps maintain a fat, full, lush plant for years to come. If left unpinched, extremely long vine-type branches will grow clear to the floor; I have seen them as long as 35 feet.

Swedish ivy, also, has two major varieties. One has solid green leaves, and the other has variegated leaves. Both varieties must be pinched regularly. If you fail to pinch them, they will begin to trail over the side of the container; the older foliage will die out, and the actively growing foliage will end up hanging at the tips of the long stems. It is so important to pinch, pinch, pinch your *Plectranthus*.

HANGING BASKETS
Flowers

To provide additional color to your houseplant collection, grow hanging baskets that produce flowers as part of their desired characteristics. One of my favorites is the *Hoya carnosa* because it is so easy to grow and takes little care. Another favorite is the *Columnea* 'Christmas Carol,' which can bloom continuously.

H. carnosa is better known as the wax plant. It can be grown on a trellis, but in a hanging basket it can be wound around and around. It needs little attention. Give the wax plant three to four hours of direct sun each day and allow it to dry considerably between waterings, even during active growth. During periods of no new growth allow the soil to become even drier. Feed sparingly at all times. The *H. carnosa* produces a wax-like, almost artificial-looking, flower cluster. Many people see a "little stem" beginning to grow from the trailing vines and, since it has no leaves, they pinch it off. They have just removed the flowering spur and, thus, the potential for flowers. After flowering occurs, pinch off only the flower head — not the stalk. The plant will bloom again and again from this point.

Columnea 'Christmas Carol' has small, dark green leaves and produces large red flowers which bloom during most of the year. The secret to keeping the trailing stems in production is pinching them back to initiate juvenile growth. This plant produces its best flowers on new growth.

Feed flowering hanging baskets with a balanced, high-phosphorus and potassium fertilizer. Look for the first number on the label to be smaller than the second and third, for example, 5-10-10 or its equivalent.

A tip: Always remove spent blossoms from your flowering hanging baskets. This will remove potential seed production and put all the energy back into growth and more flowering.

HOUSEPLANTS
Foliage Potted Plants

There is a plant that folds its leaves at night into what appears to be a pair of praying hands, and, appropriately, it is called the prayer plant. There are several varieties of prayer plant, each with various sized leaves and each with different patterns in their leaves. As a potted plant, it can add character to your collection, with its different leaf colors and trailing stems. It can be allowed to spread over the top, or to trail over the edge, of a table. The prayer plant needs filtered bright light — no full sun, or it will have bleached colors and brown tips. Keep this plant slightly moist and provide as much humidity as possible. There will be insignificant flowers produced two or three times a year.

The rabbit's foot fern is another member of my family of foliage houseplants. In fact, I call it "Harry" because of the "furry little feet" which grow over the surface of the soil and down the sides of the pot. This plant should be grown in filtered light and kept slightly moist. The rabbit's foot fern requires a high-nitrogen plant food, such as 8-7-6 or its equivalent. Foliage grows straight up from the rhizomes (the little furry feet). It can be grown in the same pot for years. In fact, if it is allowed to become extremely potbound, you will have to break the pot to get it out. If the "little feet" break off, that is all right; you can start new plants with them. Press them gently into a well-drained potting mix and keep them slightly moist. In a short time you will have many "little Harrys" to give to friends.

HOUSEPLANTS
Flowering Potted Plants

In a houseplant collection, flowering potted plants will add considerable enjoyment throughout the year. Many bloom constantly. Two groups of plants which will enhance any collection are the roses and the begonias. They both will provide hundreds of flowers over a 12-month period.

Roses grown for the indoor garden are miniature. They have been cultured from the China rose. Today there is a real interest in the hundreds of new varieties which have recently been hybridized. Some varieties are fragrant, produce double flowers, and also have beautiful lush green foliage; in addition there are many colors from which to choose.

A miniature rose requires a bright sunny window. It should be kept slightly moist, particularly during active growth. Feed it with 5-10-5, or its equivalent. Proper sanitation practices will help control many pests, such as mites, spider mites, aphids, and mealybugs. Rinse the plant with water once a week to keep it clean and to wash off the pests. Pruning practices are similar to those used with the traditional rose (see "Roses"). Prune spent flowers to at least the first set of five leaflets, where the next blooming stem will develop.

Fibrous-rooted begonias will also add bloom to a collection, as they produce profusely. The flowers vary in size and color, and, if pinched regularly, the stems can be kept from becoming "leggy." After pinching, many new shoots will develop on the lower stems. This dense growth reduces air circulation and traps humid air around the foliage, creating an ideal breeding ground for mildew, which can become a major problem on the foliage of the fibrous-rooted begonias. Pinch out one third of all the new growth. The plant won't miss it, and the increased air circulation will help control the fungus.

DISH GARDENS
Living Together

Have you ever received a dish garden as a gift? Beautiful, wasn't it? Now what does it look like? Or do you still have it? Aesthetically, dish gardens are designed to be pleasing to the eye, but practically speaking, they are not usually designed to grow compatibly. Generally, one plant likes it dry, one likes it slightly moist, and one likes it quite moist. So, no matter how you water it, something begins to die. (I'm sure there are some exceptions.)

I find the best method for maintaining a dish garden is to take it apart, put each plant in a tiny clay pot, and then place them all back in the dish. Fill the areas between the pots with peat moss or potting soil. In this way you can give each plant the right amount of water.

The other problem with dish gardens is that from little plants often come great big plants. Think of the neat little palm from the dish garden that now is four feet tall, or the wee ivy that is now five feet long. Some plants just don't belong in a dish garden.

Let me give you some pointers on how to construct your own dish garden. Because most dish garden containers do not have drainage holes, place a layer of gravel in the bottom of the container. This will help provide some drainage and aeration for the roots. Select plants that all require the same growing conditions (for example, water and light). Also, make sure they are dwarf plants, or at least small plants that will grow at a slow, steady pace. Do not stimulate new growth by over-feeding, because you want them to remain dwarf or miniature.

GARDENIA
Mist, Mist, and Mist Some More

Millions of gardenias are raised by the industry each year for the consumer market (you and me). But for some reason, after the plant comes into the home, not many of them live to be one year old. I have asked many groups the same questions: "How many have a live gardenia in their collection of plants?" About 5% raise their hands. Then I ask, "How many have *had* a gardenia in their home at one time or another?" Many hands go up, as many as 50%. Does that tell you something? It tells me either that gardenias are tough to grow, or that the consumer doesn't know how to treat them.

When you purchase a gardenia, it often has buds ready to open, and it is a fat, full plant in a small pot. The first thing most people do is to give it a big drink of water and transplant it into a larger pot. This is the beginning of the end.

Instead, let the plant become acclimated to its new environment before you ever consider transplanting. The gardenia has been growing in a greenhouse, a very humid environment. When it is taken to the "Sahara Desert" (that is how dry our homes may be in the winter), it goes into shock. The leaves begin to turn yellow and drop, and the buds fall off. Some leaves even fall while totally green. Mother Nature is trying to adjust the plant to its new home.

Second, keep the plant as humid as possible. Mist the plant as often as you can. Mist, mist, mist, and mist some more. This is one plant which requires, and will benefit from, all the misting attention you can give it. Keep the soil evenly moist and feed it with a balanced houseplant food for flowering plants. The gardenia loves the east light — about one half day of sun — but not noontime sun.

During the summer the gardenia may be placed outside in a protected area that has morning sun. New leaves will emerge and flower buds will begin to set. However, in the fall, when the plant is brought back indoors, the leaf drop cycle begins all over. Mist, mist, and mist some more!

"Oh, boy — 55° for 45 nights!"

CHRISTMAS CACTUS
A Cold-Lover

Hardly a day goes by during the Christmas season that I don't hear the question: "Grandmother's Christmas cactus always bloomed for the holidays and mine doesn't. Why?" The answer: modern technology.

Schlumbergera species flower in relation to day length and cool temperatures. Grandmother's Christmas cactus probably grew in a cool, sunny window. The night temperature in the house was probably much lower than in modern homes. Storm windows were not as efficient as the ones available today. We now have heating systems that maintain a constant, warm temperature.

I remember my grandmother telling me that there was often ice on the washbasin in the morning when she got up. This fact alone might indicate the part cold night temperatures played in the blooming of the Christmas cactus.

This plant needs night temperatures no warmer than 55 degrees for a period of 45 days or longer to trigger the flowering mechanism. Once the flowers start to develop, the night temperature is not as critical, but if cool nights are continued, it is possible to keep the plant blooming for even longer periods during the winter. So, turn down the heat. Or, do as I do. Set the Christmas cactus outside in the fall. Place it under a shrub to avoid any light frost damage. Let it remain out until just before the first real freeze. If the temperatures are cool in the fall, your Christmas cactus will bloom in time for the holidays.

In areas where the temperature is not low enough to trigger the flowering mechanism, start a night shading process in mid-September by placing the plant in total darkness (a closet will do) for a period of no less than 12 hours each night, for 40 nights.

The general care for the Christmas cactus is quite simple. Pot it in a well-drained, organic mix and allow it to dry considerably during the rest period (the period of no growth that generally occurs right after blooming stops). During active growth feed it with a low-nitrogen fertilizer, such as 15-30-15 or equivalent, and stand back and watch it bloom.

"Oh, no — not **THE CLOSET** again!"

POINSETTIAS
6:00 PM, October 1st!

The number one plant given as a gift during the holidays is the poinsettia. In its natural environment it blooms in January and February. A poinsettia that is in bloom for November and December has been "forced" by the commercial grower.

If you receive a poinsettia as a gift you can assume it has been growing in a greenhouse, where the humidity is high. It will probably drop some of its lower leaves when first coming into the house, because during the winter the humidity in our homes is very low. Don't panic. Keep the plant slightly moist and provide good, bright light. The newer varieties do not need full sun when grown as houseplants. Keep feeding the plant with a high-nitrogen food, such as 12-6-6 or equivalent. The high nitrogen will stimulate bigger and greener leaves. On June 1, prune the plant back to 50% of its height. This will remove most of the foliage and any of the colorful bracts that may still be on the plant. Strong, new shoots will begin to develop from lower down on the stems. Each branch that is pruned back usually develops at least three new stems. On July 15, pinch the growing tips out of each new shoot. Continue bright light, feed regularly according to the fertilizer label directions, and keep the plant slightly moist.

How can you make your poinsettia bloom for the Christmas season? It is simple if you have a closet with absolutely no light at night. Place the poinsettia in this closet starting at 6:00 P.M. on October 1, for a minimum of 12 hours each night, for 40 nights consecutively. Don't miss a night, and don't open the door at night to see how it is doing. (By letting in artificial light you will delay the blooming cycle.) You must remember to take the plant out of the closet each morning and place it where it will get bright light during the day. Continue this procedure until November 10, and you will have a poinsettia in bloom for the holidays.

SPIDER PLANTS
Babies and Birth Control

What makes babies on spider plants? I wish I knew. I've had a newly planted baby spider plant produce a baby in six weeks. On the other hand, I had a three-year-old plant that hadn't produced a single offspring. I have been told to let them become potbound, to repot them, to feed them, to let them dry out, to keep them moist, etc. I've even thought about getting a gynecologist to send me some fertility drugs to try on them. Nothing seems to work. I guess when they are ready to have babies, they will. Babies and flowers are spontaneously produced on long, umbilical cord-like stems.

The spider plant is one of the easiest of all houseplants to grow. It will put up with neglect as well as any other plant. I have seen spider plants in restaurants and hotel lobbies that are really suffering from neglect, but they keep hanging on. I have seen spider plants bursting out of their pots, but they keep growing.

The spider plant needs a well-draining soil, slightly moist conditions, and a high-nitrogen plant food, such as 12-6-6 or its equivalent. If the plant is in too much sun, it will show bleaching of the beautiful green color in the leaves. If the soil is allowed to dry too much between waterings, brown tips may occur. Increasing the humidity will help eliminate brown tips. If all conditions are right the spider plant will begin to produce babies — maybe.

GERANIUMS
Roots Up and Shoots Down?

Every year on Mother's Day geraniums become the number one selling plant in the U.S.A. At the end of the growing season they probably are the number one discarded plant. They needn't be. Geraniums can be saved from year to year by either of two relatively simple methods.

If they have been grown in the garden over summer, they can be dug, pruned back by one-third, and potted up for growing in a bright, sunny but cool window. Water sparingly and feed with 15-30-15 or its equivalent. Geraniums kept in these conditions will continue to grow and flower. It will be necessary to pinch or prune them back several times during the winter to avoid leggy growth.

Another method of saving geraniums that has proven successful time and time again is to store them. In the fall, before the first killing frost, dig the plants from the ground. Pinch off any flowers or flower buds but leave all the stems and foliage. The stems contain the needed moisture and growth buds for the next season. Shake the soil from the roots and place each plant upside down in a brown paper bag. Fasten the bag with a string so the roots stick out and are exposed to the air. Hang the bags, with the roots at the top, in the garage or basement (in a cool area), but not where they will freeze. Forty to forty-five degrees is excellent for winter storage.

In late February take the bags down and remove the withered plants. Prune back any damaged roots and clip the tops down to eight or ten inches. Pot in well-drained potting soil and thoroughly soak the soil with water containing a starter solution of fertilizer for flowering plants.

Keep the plants in a cool area, in moderate light (no direct sun), until new growth begins. This may take two to three weeks. Once new growth shows bright green color, it is time to move the plants to a bright, sunny but cool window. You will have beautiful, stocky geraniums back in bloom for Mother's Day. The success rate for this method is about eight out of ten.

"See you guys next month!"

HOUSEPLANTS FOR THE TRAVELER
Gone a Lot?

Many people can't be at home to take care of houseplants and yet they would appreciate something green and growing during the short times they are at home. If you are one of these people, don't despair. There are houseplants for you. Select those that just sit there and take care of themselves.

The place to start, for the traveler, is with plants that need water only when you are home to give it to them.

Cactuses may be the solution. Most cactuses will put up with considerable neglect, especially when it comes to watering, or the lack of it. There are hundreds from which to choose. My favorites include, but are not limited to: the old-man cactus, urchin cactus, pincushion cactus, and the opuntia. All of these love a sunny window and need very little water. During the winter, if they are allowed to be in cold temperatures (in the low 40's), they will set flowers and bloom. The secret to success with cactuses is neglect.

Besides cactuses, another favorite is the ponytail palm. This plant has a bulb-like structure at its base, from which a wispy growth originates. It makes an excellent specimen plant in the home because it requires no direct sun. Water the ponytail plant every other month, and keep it in a very small pot in relation to the size of the bulb.

Sansevierias are another group of plants that are great for the absentee gardener. They are one of the hardiest of all houseplants. You may know them as the snake plant, or the mother-in-law's tongue. They need indirect light, watering about once a month, and feeding once every two or three months. In fact, I let one snake plant dry for six months, and three weeks after I gave it a drink it bloomed.

You too can travel and still enjoy houseplants. Just pick the right plants.

"Green leaves — that's all I ask!"

FUN PLANTS FROM THE KITCHEN
The Pits

It's the pits! But from the pits comes a fun collection of houseplants. The two pits I refer to are avocado and citrus. Both can be grown into fantastic houseplants that last for years. In fact, they both could become nice trees for the living room.

Start with the avocado. First you eat the avocado, but save the pit. Partially embed four toothpicks, one into each side, about half way down the pit, to create a "helicopter" look. Set the pit, point up, in a glass of water, supported by its toothpick "rotors," so that the bottom is submerged about one third. Place the glass on a shelf out of the sun and add water regularly. Be patient. The pit may crack open in a week or so and send out roots and shoots. But as I said, be patient. There is no way to tell how ripe the pit was when it was harvested, so this may take as long as three months. Once the roots and shoots begin to develop, remove the picks and transplant the entire pit into a well-drained potting soil, with one third of the pit above the soil. Water, feed, and keep the new plant in a sunny window. Before long, you will have a tree in your home.

The citruses include oranges, grapefruits, and lemons. Save the seeds after eating the fruit, soak them in water for 24 hours, and plant them one-half inch deep in a sterilized potting soil. Keep the soil slightly moist, and in just a few days the seeds will begin to grow. Start one seed per pot for best results. After growth begins, keep the new plant where it will get one-half day of bright sun. Avoid noontime sun; it will burn the leaves. Feed the plant regularly with a high-nitrogen houseplant food, and then "back off and watch it grow."

From both the avocado and citrus you will grow a beautiful foliage plant — but don't hold your breath until they flower and fruit.

MORE FUN PLANTS FROM THE KITCHEN
The Sweets

Two other plants that can be added to your houseplant collection from the kitchen garbage are the pineapple and sweet potato.

The pineapple makes a great foliage houseplant, because it is from the bromeliad family. Bromeliads are excellent for a home that does not have an abundance of sun. When you are ready to prepare the pineapple for eating, put on a pair of gloves and place the pineapple between your knees. Clamp tightly and twist out the top. A long, tapered, carrot-like center will come out with the top. Cut off this center core about two inches below the bottom of the foliage. Plant it in a well-drained potting mix and keep it slightly moist. After growth begins, water sparingly and feed with any high-nitrogen houseplant food (10-5-5 or its equivalent). Clip off any brown or damaged tips on the foliage. You now have a pineapple plant for your collection — but don't expect it to produce a new pineapple.

The sweet potato makes a vining-type plant and is extremely easy to grow. Once the sweet potato starts to sprout, it is no longer good eating but it can be suspended in water, with toothpicks as supports, and grown as a houseplant. The potato will begin to root and will develop a long vine. Continue to grow this plant by adding fresh water weekly. Pinching the tips of the vine will produce several side shoots and develop into an attractive, cascading plant. Eventually, the potato will run out of energy and begin to die. At this point, throw it out and start all over.

OUTDOORS

"Guess their plants got out of hand."

LANDSCAPE PLANTING
Plan Before You Plant

The phrase "Plan Before You Plant" has been used in gardening for years and refers to the total planning process: studying the soil, selecting the plant material, determining the lighting conditions, and evaluating the growing environment. It applies to the planting of a new landscape, as well as vegetable, annual, and perennial gardens. From little plants often come great big plants. Remember the five little plants that were placed along the foundation in front of the house. And now, you can't see out the picture window! This is a simple case of not planning.

At the start of the planning process you should test the soil for pH (soil acidity). This is an important factor because some plants need acid soil and some like a more alkaline condition. Soils can be made more alkaline by applying lime and can be made more acid by applying sulfur. Proper drainage is important as well. Some plants like moist root systems while others will die in wet conditions. You can improve drainage by adding sand, organic matter, and gypsum. It may be necessary to consult a soils specialist to determine alternatives. Organic matter must be added to the soil before planting, in the form of peat moss or compost. Organic matter helps hold nutrients in the soil as well as improves drainage.

Other factors in plant selection are also critical. Does the plant like sun, partial sun, or shade? How big will it ultimately get? Can you keep it in bounds? What is the color of the foliage? Of the flower? Is it compatible with other plants in the landscape? With the great selection of plant material available today virtually all conditions can be met.

Finally, consider the effect of seasonal changes on the plants you select. Some plants can tolerate cold winter winds; others may burn severely. Winter protection may be an alternative if you have the time and are so inclined, but why not put the right plant in the first time?

As you can see, planning is important. By giving proper consideration to the planning and planting process you will avoid many mistakes made by novice landscapers.

PLANTING
A 50¢ Plant in a $5 Hole

The philosophy of a "50¢ plant in a $5 hole" refers to the importance of proper preparation of the site and environment before planting. Of course, to start with, you have to select the right plant. Make sure you choose a plant that is suited to the location in relation to sun or shade. Then look at the drainage and moisture level of the soil, since some plants like it damp and others don't.

But once you have selected a suitable plant, the preparation of the hole itself is of prime importance. The plant is going to spend the rest of its life there, so spend time and energy doing it right. Dig the hole extra wide and deep. It should be at least twice the width of the ball or container, to allow for better root penetration and amending of the soil. The hole should be one-and-one-half times the depth of the ball or container. This will allow you to check the drainage and remove all debris or rocks to encourage deeper rooting. For roses I dig the hole four to five times the depth of the roots to provide for excellent drainage and for the eventual development of the tap root that is so important in rose culture.

After digging the hole, you should add organic matter — about 50% by volume — in the form of peat moss or compost. This must be stirred into the soil taken from the hole. Organic matter in a layer by itself will act as a sponge and hold too much moisture. Nutrients in the form of slow release fertilizers may be thoroughly mixed with this backfill.

Synthetic burlap, such as nylon or plastic, must be removed before planting. It will never decay and the roots will not be able to become properly established. Also, remove plants from their containers. Measure the depth of the ball and backfill the hole with the prepared mix so the top of the ball is slightly above the level of the top of the hole. This allows for the settling of soil beneath the plant as it grows.

Place the plant in the hole and then step back. Look at the plant to make sure the best side faces the desired direction. Begin backfilling the hole with the prepared mix. Tamp the fill around the ball and water thoroughly to remove any air pockets that might cause drying of the roots. Form the soil into a dish around the rim of the hole to provide a water reservoir and continue watering the plant as needed.

Now you have put a "50¢ plant in a $5 hole" and you will have a "$5 plant" shortly!

"But I only bought ONE of each!"

TOOLS FOR THE BEGINNING GARDENER
Don't Buy Out the Store

For the first-time gardener or new homeowner, selecting the right tools for the garden can be a frustrating experience. Garden centers and hardware stores have hundreds to choose from, but there are a few basic tools that have multipurpose uses.

You need a garden spading fork. This is a short-handled tool with tines to do the work. It can be used to dig or spade the garden in the spring, to dig holes for planting, and to break up big clods of soil. Do not use it to pry debris, such as stones or roots, from the ground. The tines may break.

A garden rake is necessary and comes in two basic designs. Both have long handles and a comb-like head. The flat head rake is rigid in construction and is excellent for raking and leveling planting areas. The bowhead rake is somewhat more flexible and durable. The choice is yours.

Although hoes come in many sizes and shapes, a general gardening hoe will do. It can be used to make trenches for planting, to chop the weeds around plants, and to break up clods of compacted soil. Another hoe I recommend for the gardener is the scuffle hoe. It comes in several styles and is used to eliminate weeds from the garden with as little work as possible. Purchase a file to keep the cutting edge sharp on any hoe that you choose.

For major digging projects like tree and shrub planting, purchase a medium-point, general purpose shovel. It has a long, straight handle which makes digging easier, and the handle can also be used to check the depth of the hole. A great tool!

Now I know that you will be tempted to purchase many more tools, but don't. Get to know your garden tasks before you invest in equipment. Buy quality tools which will last you a lifetime if you take care of them. Don't lean too hard on the handles and don't lend anything to neighbors.

More tools to look at as you become more experienced include: hand cultivators, tillers, leaf blowers, nursery spades, etc. Before you purchase, check for quality. The cheapest tool is usually not the best.

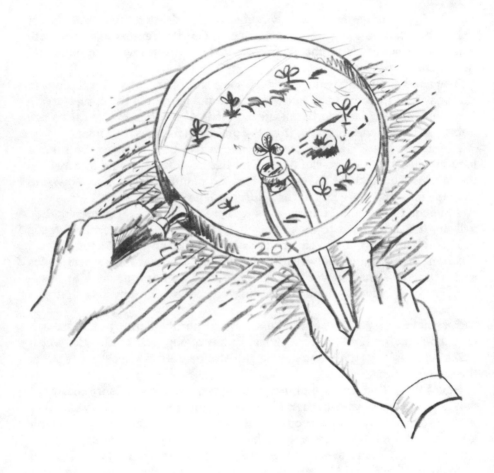

POSTAGE STAMP GARDENING
A Collector's Paradise

Postage stamp gardening doesn't mean planting postage stamps in your garden! It means to grow carefully selected small or dwarf plants in a small area.

First, let's define *dwarf* and *dwarfed* as they refer to plants. The term *dwarf* describes an inherent characteristic, not a result of cultural practices, while *dwarfed* characteristics are those that have been induced by cultural practices and environmental conditions. Both terms are descriptions given to the size of one plant in relation to the size of another plant, generally within a species. The mugo pine and the Swiss mountain pine are of the same species, but the mugo would be referred to as *dwarf* because it is the smaller and more compact of the two.

With the development of many new varieties of plants the horticultural industry has made postage stamp gardening quite easy. Look in any catalog or visit your local garden center and you will find a vast selection of plants labeled "Dwarf" from which to choose, some of which will remain very compact and some of which will need pruning to keep them compact. There are both evergreen and deciduous varieties, including miniature trees. The decision is yours, depending on the type of garden you want.

The growing of a postage stamp garden is basically the same as any other. You prepare the soil, plant the plants, and feed and water. The difference between postage stamp gardening and any other is not only in the selection of dwarf material, but also in the pruning practices. You must perform proper pruning to keep plants dwarfed that would tend not to be.

PRUNING TOOLS
Do You Really Need an Arsenal?

The selection of hand pruning tools depends on the types of plants that you are growing. Each pruning practice has a specific tool to do the job. You would not use a chain saw to cut suckers off a dogwood tree or to prune your rose bushes. Selecting the right tool will make the pruning task easier.

In light pruning, select hand pruning shears which are constructed to cut off small twigs with the use of one hand. The two styles of hand shears are scissor action and anvil blade runner. Scissor action pruners give a clean cut and generally can be used in tighter areas than the anvil blade. The anvil blade can be used to cut larger branches without springing open the jaws of the pruning head. It is human nature to try to cut a branch that is too large for a one-handed clipper. When we put the other hand to work, this force or pressure is more than the pruner is designed for, and we end up purchasing a new pair of hand pruning shears. When I purchase equipment I look for a pruner that fits and feels good in my hand. Then I put it back on the shelf and buy the next size larger.

Heavy pruning jobs, such as the removal of branches on dogwoods, crabapples, etc., can be accomplished with a pair of loppers. These are long-handled shears that are constructed similarly to the hand shears. There are both scissor type and anvil blade. Make sure the handles are of the finest quality wood or steel. Weak parts will break easily. If the branch is too large to be easily cut with the lopper, use a saw.

If you have ever tried to cut a branch off a tree with a carpenter's saw, you know that it works on the push. Three pushes in an upward motion and you are tired out. The hand pruning saw works on the pull. The weight of the hands and arms do all the work. The best type of pruning saw is the curved-blade handsaw. Keep the pruning saw clean, well oiled, and sharp. It will last a lifetime.

As you become more expert at pruning you may wish to have hedge shears, pole pruners, chain saws, etc., but don't invest in these items until you really need them.

PRUNING FLOWERING SHRUBS AND TREES
Caution!

You don't even have to know the name of the plant you are about to prune if you know when it blooms. If there is any doubt as to the blooming cycle, just let it grow for a complete season and observe when it blooms.

Plants that bloom in the spring — June or before — generally bloom on last year's growth. So if a plant that blooms in the spring needs light pruning, do it just as the flowers fade and before the seeds start to develop. This way the seeds do not form, and all the energy is put back into growth which produces the blooms for the next spring. If pruning of spring-blooming plants is done before the bloom, no flowering will occur. Plants that bloom after June, bloom on the current season's growth. So light pruning of summer-blooming plants is done in the early part of the growing season to stimulate better growth for flowering during the current season.

Severe pruning of nearly all plants needs to be done in the early spring, without regard to the blooming season. Cool, moist spring weather allows better bud development before hot, parching conditions dry out the plant tissue. With many plants, if severe pruning is done in the fall, damage may occur during winter, because you are cutting off much of the food reserves that are still stored in the upper portion of the plants. One possible reason for severe fall pruning is to create dwarf growth in the spring. The plant will have less stored food to initiate growth.

Dead or dying branches should be pruned immediately, no matter what time of year it is. This practice removes insect-infested wood and just might stop diseases.

HEDGE PRUNING
Can You See Your Neighbor?

Most of us who grow hedges on our property lines grow them so we can keep our privacy. But after about five years, we may be sitting in the yard, and what do we see through the bottom of the hedge? Our neighbors! This is a case of improper pruning, not the fault of the plant.

Pruning techniques for hedges depend on whether you want a natural or a formal, sheared look. Plants such as forsythia and spirea need to be thinned out to allow juvenile growth constantly to emerge from the ground. Otherwise, the taller, older growth will create a thin look by blocking out light to the younger shoots. Each year, simply remove one-fourth of all of the oldest canes right after bloom. This will enable the plant to regenerate itself every four years and retain its density.

Formal hedges are another story. It is essential to prune the hedge in an A-frame shape, keeping the top slightly narrower than the base. This will allow light to reach the lower leaves and provide for growth. If pruning is done in a vertical fashion on the sides, or in a V-shape, light cannot reach the lowest leaves, and they will begin to drop.

It is not difficult to maintain the flat, even look of the top of the formal hedge. Put a pole in the ground at each end of the hedge and draw a string from end to end. This will be the straight cutting line. It is almost impossible to make a straight cut along the entire hedge by using the eyeball method. I don't care how careful you are, you will end up with one end higher than the other and an uneven top.

To prune natural hedges you will need a pair of lopping shears to cut out the older growth. For formal hedges you will need hedge clippers. Buy the best quality available. Power operated shears come in electric and gas models. Caution: when using electric shears, don't cut the cord!

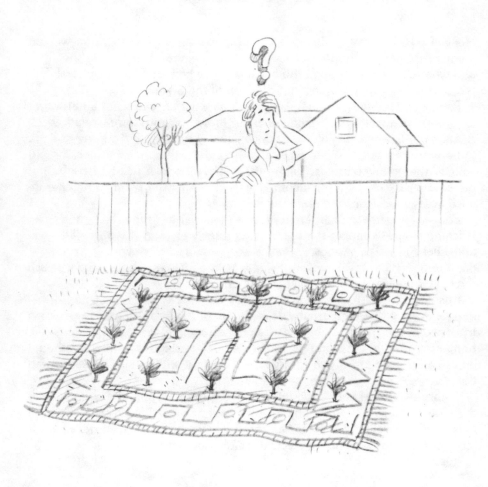

MULCHES
A Blanket on the Soil

The use of a mulch can probably provide more benefits than any other single gardening practice. A mulch is nothing but a covering over the surface of the soil. It helps conserve moisture; it keeps down the weeds; it prevents great fluctuations of temperature around the roots; it discourages damage to roots due to cultivation, and it provides aesthetic appeal.

Suggested mulches include pine bark chips, wood chips, pine needles, salt hay, different sizes of gravel, and even newspaper. Buckwheat hulls and cocoa hulls look natural and are decorative for perennial gardens. Do not use buckwheat hulls in a windy area; they will blow away. Cocoa hulls will provide a fragrance for a few days that will make you think you are in your favorite chocolate shop.

With a layer of mulch, less evaporation occurs, thereby conserving precious moisture during dry periods. A mulch blocks out light, thus preventing the growth of weeds and eliminating the need for cultivation, which can damage the root system of the plants. A mulch also maintains a more even soil temperature.

Aesthetically, mulches can be very pleasing. To dress up the landscape, many natural mulches, such as pine bark, redwood chips, washed gravel, or crushed granite, may be used. The selection of a mulch for appearance depends on the effect desired. Use a dark-colored mulch such as pine bark chips if you want the plant to take on a natural appearance, blending in with the environment. If you want the plant to stand out as an individual, use a light-colored mulch such as granite or washed gravel.

WINTER PROTECTION
Brrr, It's Cold!

In many areas it is necessary to provide winter protection for outdoor plants. This is for the purpose of keeping the cold winter winds from drying out the leaves, or to eliminate snow load damage.

In regions where the soil freezes and stays frozen for a period of time, evergreen plants can suffer from desiccation, particularly the broadleaf varieties such as rhododendrons, azaleas, and hollies. When the ground freezes, the available water that would normally supply the plant is frozen also. Because of this, the plant cannot take up moisture for transpiration and photosynthesis. During daylight, the plant needs water for these functions. Without water the cells in the leaves begin to dehydrate and scorch symptoms appear.

There are two methods that may alleviate this problem. One is to mulch around the plants, which helps prevent deep freezing of the soil, and the other is to put up a screen to protect the plant from wind. Wind pulls the moisture out of the foliage, creating desiccation. Screening is usually done with burlap, either brown or green. (I have always found green burlap to be slightly more pleasing to the eye.) An alternative to burlap is to spray the foliage with an antidesiccant. This is a coating material applied to the foliage to seal off the cells, reducing water loss by transpiration. The newer formulations of antidesiccants do work if properly applied.

To prevent snow loads on prized plants, build a shelter over them. A caution on construction of a shelter or burlap screen: if you have an underground irrigation system in the area make sure you know where the pipes are located. Otherwise, next spring, you may discover an "Old Faithful" where a pipe was punctured.

PERENNIALS
A Symphony in the Garden

To have a symphony of bloom for the entire growing season, plant perennial flowers. There are a multitude of perennials that will make your garden play like an orchestra. As the violins finish, the flutes will take over. As the bleeding hearts finish blooming, the phlox will begin. That is what a properly designed perennial garden will do — as one flower finishes its blooming assignment, the next perennial begins to bloom. You can also have many flowers blooming at the same time.

A perennial is a herbaceous plant that annually dies back to the ground, but then continues its life cycle for at least three more years. Those that complete the life cycle in only two years are known as biennials.

To plan a perennial garden, start with selections that begin blooming early in the season. Columbine, bleeding heart, and true lavender are just a few possible selections. Mid-season bloomers include fern-leaved yarrow, Canterbury bells, dusty miller, and iris. Late bloomers could be chrysanthemums, in many varieties, border carnations, and shasta daisies. Since there are so many perennials to select from, no one else will have quite the same garden as yours.

General care of the perennial garden is quite simple. Feed with a 5-10-5 or equivalent, remove spent flowers, and water during extremely dry periods. In late fall, clean up the garden, cut back dead foliage, and you are basically ready for next year.

"It's great to be a champion."

ROSES
A Prize Winner

The care of roses starts with proper planting. Roses love a sunny environment with a well-drained soil, and it is crucial, for their overall development and longevity, to prepare the soil properly. Dig an extra-deep hole for planting — four to five times the depth of the root system. This will enable the rose to grow a healthy tap root. Mix by volume as much as 50% organic matter, such as peat moss or compost, with the backfill. Bonemeal should also be mixed in to provide phosphorus and trace element nutrients. Fill the hole with backfill to the proper planting depth. Complete the planting and water thoroughly.

As new growth begins, the care becomes critical. Problems like blackspot, mildew, aphids, Japanese beetles, mites, and thrips can destroy the blooming potential. All of these pests can be controlled with the appropriate pesticides. *Read the label.*

Pruning practices on hybrid tea roses are important. In early spring, prune the taller canes back to 12-15 inches above the ground. Take care to remove any interfering (crossing) canes and those that are growing into the center of the plant. This pruning will open the plant to more sunlight and air circulation, which will help prevent diseases. After the spring bloom, prune back the spent flowering canes. Be sure to prune back to just above the first set of five leaflets. Better yet, further down on the cane, prune back to above a five-leaflet set that is pointing to the outside of the plant. This will cause a new cane to grow up and out for better light.

In late fall or early winter, prune just enough off the top of the rose plant to prevent an "ice lollipop" from forming if a winter storm should occur. The weight of ice can split the cane off at the base of the plant. Do not do severe pruning in the fall; there is much food stored in the upper parts of the plant which is necessary for successful overwintering.

HYDRANGEAS
A Chameleon

A common question from gardeners concerning the big-leaved hydrangea is, "Why has my hydrangea changed its flower color? When I received it, it was pink and now it is blue!" The answer lies in the soil. The color is related to the pH of the soil, or soil acidity. Soils that are extremely acid will produce deep blue flowers and those that are closer to alkaline will produce pink flowers. If you keep the soil pH between 5.0 and 5.5, the color will be blue; if you raise it to 6.0 to 7.0, the color will be pink.

To encourage and deepen the blue color, use aluminum sulfate, mixing it with water and watering the plant with this solution every two weeks for three or four applications. This will need to be done annually if there is a lack of aluminum in the soil. Most soils contain some aluminum, but it may not be available to the plant if the soil pH is extremely acid.

To raise the pH to provide the pink color, add regular agricultural lime to the soil in the spring and fall, at the rate of three to five pounds per 100 square feet. This procedure may need to be repeated annually also. Pink or blue is up to you.

BULB PLANTING
Who Dug Them Up?

Each fall billions of bulbs, such as tulips, daffodils, and hyacinths, are planted to provide flowers for the following spring. Shortly after planting, some gardeners may find many of them lying on the surface of the soil, as if someone had dug them up. Don't blame the kids next door; it was most likely a rodent, such as a squirrel or chipmunk, which can be discouraged from digging by several reliable methods.

Mothballs can be planted along with the bulbs. The odor acts as a repellent. When planting the bulbs, dig the hole a little deeper than normal, stir in bonemeal, and then place a mothball in the bottom of the hole. Cover it with a thin layer of soil and finish planting the bulb at its proper depth. When the rodent starts to dig up the bulb, it will get a whiff of the mothball, and, hopefully, back away.

A wire mesh screen, such as hardware cloth, can be laid over the planted bulb bed to prevent digging. However, if this method is used, you must remember to remove the mesh in the spring before the bulbs emerge.

The use of animal and rodent repellents scattered over the surface of the soil is another method of protecting bulbs. The disadvantage of these repellents is that they must be replenished after it rains.

An additional help may be to plant the bulbs just before the ground is ready to freeze. When the soil is frozen the rodents won't dig them up.

GROUND COVERS
A Useful Blanket

Living ground covers include a great many varieties. They can be vines, low-growing shrubs, perennials, or even herbs. They are used to fill in large expansive areas, areas such as slopes that might be hard to maintain, or narrow growing areas that would be tough to mow. They are unbelievably versatile. There are species of plants that will grow either in the sun, in the shade, or in dry or wet soils.

Ground covers should be selected with care. Some are extremely slow-growing and some are very aggressive. Ivy, planted as a ground cover, will not only tend to take over a large area, but will climb trees and buildings. Bamboo planted on a slope to control erosion will probably come up through the asphalt driveway.

The secret of making the ground cover perform the function desired is in the planting. Spacing properly is essential. If you plant *Pachysandra* under the big maple tree, plant the transplants or rooted cuttings no farther apart than the span of a hand. Plant one cutting at the tip of the little finger and another at the tip of the thumb. Planting farther apart to save money will only result in disappointment and potentially a weed bed. Mulches can be used to cover the soil between the plants to conserve moisture and help keep down the weeds.

There are several preemergent weed controls that are useful in ground-cover beds. *Read the label* to be sure that the preemergent control can be used around the specific ground cover.

ANNUALS
Billions of Blossoms

Annuals are those plants that complete their life cycle in one season. They germinate, grow, flower, set seed, and mature in one year. Annuals can be used to give color to the deck, window box, or landscape planting, and can be used as cut flowers.

When you plant annual flowers in the garden in the springtime, you have great expectations for blooms all summer long. Your dreams will come true if you follow the proper procedures. To start the annual flower garden, prepare the soil as you would for any other garden. Add organic matter and fertilizer, such as 5-10-5 or equivalent, and spade the garden to a depth of eight inches or more.

If you grow your own seedlings, fine, but if you are purchasing transplants, be sure that they are properly labeled. There is nothing more disappointing than planting what you thought were red petunias and finding out they are white. If some of the plants are in bloom at the time you purchase them, then of course you can tell the color. But when you get the plants home and planted, pinch out the flowers. The removal of the flowers will allow the plants to become rooted into the soil so they can tolerate summer weather. Once the plants become established they will go back into bloom, and your garden is complete. Almost, that is. As the summer continues, spend time with your annuals and pinch out the spent blossoms. This will put the energy that would be used to make seeds back into flower production. Feed annuals with a water soluble fertilizer, such as 15-30-15 or its equivalent, according to the label directions. Annuals are big eaters.

"Now I'll have the best lawn on the block!"

LAWN
Starting from Scratch

If you want the best lawn on the block, then do it right from the beginning. It won't happen on its own. The establishment of a new lawn takes planning and work. Study the area, check the drainage and soil conditions, select the right seed, and prepare the soil properly for planting.

To study the area, check the lighting conditions. You may have sun, partial sun, or shade. No single grass will survive under all these conditions. Some grasses like sun and some like shade.

Examine the soil. If there is a drainage problem, correct it before going any further. Also, know the type of soil. If the soil is sandy, organic matter in the form of peat moss or compost will be needed. If the soil is a clay type, organic matter and gypsum will loosen the soil particles and allow for better root penetration as the grass becomes established.

Do a soil pH test to determine if lime is needed. Lime will change soil acidity and make it more alkaline. Fertilizer should be added at the recommended rates for new seeding.

Select the proper seed. There is a big difference in the quality of lawns made of bluegrass, and those made of coarse fescue. Check with your local Cooperative Extension office for the variety best suited for your conditions.

Soil preparation includes the incorporation of all the needed ingredients from the beginning, not after the fact. Spread the organic matter, lime, fertilizer, gypsum, whatever is needed, and spade or rototill the ingredients to a depth of at least eight inches. This will loosen the soil and mix the amendments to a depth that will be valuable to the grass roots.

Rake the planting area to remove any debris and provide a smooth seeding area. Spread the seed at the recommended rate and rake lightly once again. This will slightly cover the seed with soil. If you have a roller, roll the seeded bed, and then turn on the sprinkler. Once water has been applied, germination starts. Keep the soil slightly moist at all times and continue watering until the seeds are well established. You will now have a start on the best lawn on the block.

LAWN MOWING
A Cut or a Trim

Probably no single chore is disliked more by homeowners than mowing the lawn — maybe because it needs to be done so often. You go round and round the same piece of property, over and over. Even if you change direction, it's still the same.

The frequency of mowing depends on the season, type of grass, how much fertilizer was applied, and just how manicured you want the lawn to look.

Bluegrass, fescue, and rye grow best during cool, moist weather. During hot periods, Mother Nature slows their growth to protect them, since they are primarily cool-season grasses. This means you will have to mow more often during the spring and fall than during the summer.

Some grasses grow faster than others. The new, improved, perennial rye grasses will grow faster than most bluegrasses. Consequently, if you have a lawn with rye grass in the mix, you will need to mow more often.

Of course, a starved lawn will not grow as much as one that is well-fed, no matter what grass you have. Feeding is up to you. (See "Lawn Feeding")

How do you want your lawn to look? Frequent mowing will keep all the grasses looking their best. If there are several different varieties in the lawn mix, you will need to adjust your mowing practices to the fastest grower. Generally, during the spring and fall, mowing should be done every few days. During the summer less frequent mowing is required.

My philosophy in mowing is never to mow off more than one third of the leaf blade at any one time. If more is removed, the crown of the plant may be exposed to the strong sun which can cause burnout.

During spring and fall, the cool-season grasses can be mowed at one to two inches in height. During the hot summer, raise the mowing height to two to three inches. The taller mowing height will allow the grass to cope better with the hot, dry periods.

LAWN WATERING
A Big Drink!

The debate, whether lawns should or should not be watered, still goes on. Much research indicates the value of irrigation, if used properly. How many times have you driven around the neighborhood during rainy weather and seen an irrigation system running? Many, I'm sure. My guess is that the owner has an automatic system. In other words, the lawn gets a drink, whether it needs it or not.

A general rule for the lawn is to supply one inch of water per week during the growing season. This includes Mother Nature's contributions. How can you tell the amount of water that has been delivered from either irrigation or rainfall? Install a rain gauge and keep accurate records. If the lawn has not received the required amount, and the grass is beginning to show stress, turn on the irrigation system. There will be periods when no additional watering is needed, so shut off your sprinklers and save your money.

To determine the amount of water your irrigation system is delivering, place a small can in the sprinkler pattern and measure the amount of water collected after a given period of time. You will be amazed at how long it takes to sprinkle one inch of water. Be sure to let the sprinkler run long enough.

Always water long and deep. This practice will develop a strong, deep root system, and eventually you may not have to water at all. Of course, if water begins to run off into the street, your soil has taken in all it can. Short periods of irrigation moisten only the surface soil. This encourages the grass to develop shallow roots and thus become dependent on irrigation.

LAWN WEED CONTROL
It's the Only Green I Have!

What do dandelion, plantain, chickweed, clover, wild onion, and crabgrass have in common? They are all weeds that invade the lawn. In fact, if you look closely, they might comprise the entire lawn. Be careful before you kill them off; you could end up with some v / bare spots.

The broadleaf weeds — dandelion, plantain, and chickweed — crowd out the desirable grasses. These weeds are controlled by specially formulated broadleaf weed killers. *Read the label.*

Some gardeners love to spend the growing season down on their hands and knees pulling dandelions, but the weeds always seem to grow back, usually twice as big. The problem with hand control of weeds that produce a tap root is that if the root is not cut off deep enough under the soil, two shoots replace the one.

Chickweed and plantain can be hand pulled if done before they can reseed themselves. Clover can be hand-controlled, also.

Controlling wild onion requires a different approach. They are produced from bulbs that develop underground. Hand pulling is a smelly job and very ineffective. If one bulblet is allowed to remain, up it comes again. The use of a broadleaf weed killer will be somewhat effective, but a second application will be necessary.

Crabgrass is a grassy weed which can be stopped with a preemergent or postemergent control. *Read the label* and understand that some preemergent controls can be used, and some cannot, when a new lawn has just been planted from seed. Crabgrass needs to be controlled at any stage before it goes to seed, since one plant can produce up to 300,000 seeds.

LAWN FEEDING
A Menu and Agenda

Choosing the best method of feeding the lawn starts with reading the fertilizer label. If you have visited a garden center lately you have seen the many brands and formulas of fertilizers available. Each basically says it's the best. Which one should you use?

The choice of fertilizer depends on what you want to accomplish, what time of year it is, and what type of grass you are growing. If you want to establish a strong root system, you would most likely use a high-phosphorus and potassium fertilizer. If you want to push leaf growth you would use a high-nitrogen food.

There are many formulas from which to choose. Some have a nitrogen source that is totally chemical base, some are 50% organic or slow release, and some are 100% organic or totally slow release. I prefer to use a nitrogen fertilizer in the spring that will stimulate leaf growth early enough to crowd out the weeds. Then I switch to a slower release nitrogen fertilizer that will feed the lawn over the summer months. Do not apply fertilizer during the hot months. It will stimulate growth that is more susceptible to disease problems. In the fall, the use of a high-phosphorus fertilizer, containing a moderate amount of nitrogen, will develop a stronger, deeper root system and will encourage some leaf growth.

Research has shown that if only one application of fertilizer is to be used, the later fall application would be the one to consider. A basic lawn feeding program would consist of one application in early spring, one in late spring, and one in the fall.

The amount of fertilizer used depends on the type of grass, because some require more than others. A zoysia lawn requires about one-third less nitrogen than a bluegrass lawn.

Read the label for the rates and the methods of application.

LAWNS
Keep Off the Grass?

"Keep off the grass" is a sign we often see displayed on turf areas. This is quite understandable if the sign marks an area under repair, but many more times than not it is posted on well-established turf grasses that can take some wear and tear. When millions of dollars are spent annually for growing turf why can't it be utilitarian *as well as* beautiful to look at?

A lawn can be picture-perfect and still be walked on if the right grass is planted. Study the available varieties: some are best for sun or shade; some are disease resistant; some will take more foot traffic than others. Check with your local garden center or your Cooperative Extension Association for the variety that is best for you.

In general, bluegrass can take considerable punishment, though not as much as tall fescue, which is the grass often used on athletic fields. The new improved perennial ryegrass is compatible with both the tall fescue and the bluegrass, although it grows somewhat faster than the bluegrass.

Choose the proper seed mix for your needs and follow a program of proper maintenance: water, feed, mow, and weed. Then you can take down your sign that says "Keep off the grass."

FRUIT TREES
June Drop

"June drop" is a term often heard from growers of peaches, pears, apricots, and apples. It means just what it says: the fruit falls off in June. In the industry, this is disastrous. If all the fruit falls off before maturing, the grower will have nothing to harvest and sell. June drop can be just as disappointing to the home gardener.

In the spring, during the time that fruit is setting on the tree, there is usually plenty of moisture in the soil and the air temperature is cool. The plant sets its fruit and all is fine. A spray schedule is commenced to control insects and diseases. But then in June the air temperature begins to rise and the soil becomes dry. Now the plant has all that fruit but is not able to supply the moisture needed for development. In response, Mother Nature sends a signal throughout the plant, telling it she has overproduced and, in order to save the tree, the fruit must go. The problem here is, the plant has no way to know how much fruit should be dropped, so it drops it all.

Commercially, there are thinning agents that are sprayed on the tree shortly after fruit set, to cause a percentage of the fruit to fall. This is rather tricky, though, because if one ounce too much is used, all the fruit may drop.

For the home gardener, hand thinning is best. Simply remove all the fruit between the span of a hand. Stretch out your hand and proceed down the branches, removing every fruit between the tip of the little finger and the thumb. With peaches, leave a pair of fruit at the little finger position and a pair at the thumb position. Do this to all the branches until you have pairs of peaches all over the tree. You will then have mechanically thinned the fruit and your reward from Mother Nature — all other factors being equal — will be the best fruit on the block.

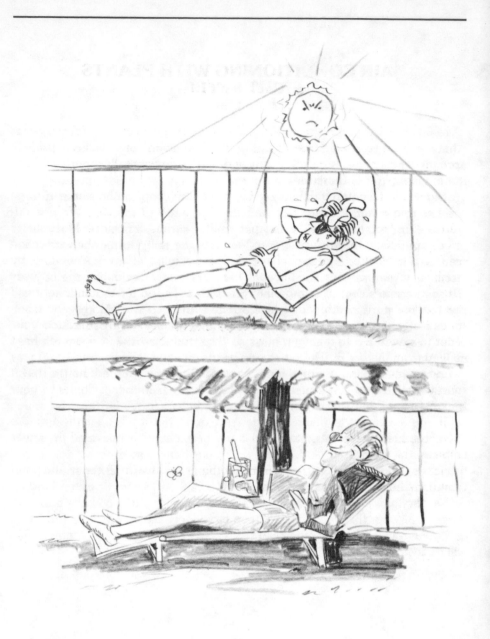

AIR CONDITIONING WITH PLANTS
Cool, Isn't It!

As you travel through the countryside, look at the many old farm houses that have large shade trees planted close to them, and observe the tall hedges of evergreens on the north and west sides of the property. Those trees were planted there for a purpose.

Big shade trees provide wonderful air conditioning. Stand under a large tree during a hot summer day and then go out into the sun. What a difference! In fact, there can be as much as 20 degrees difference. Most shade trees are deciduous (dropping their leaves in the fall). During the winter the sun is not blocked by the foliage and a warming effect is provided by sunlight which reaches the house. There are many deciduous shade trees from which to select. If a large evergreen tree is used for shading, light will be blocked out in both winter and summer and you will not receive a balanced effect. Wind screens provided by evergreens will help reduce your energy needs by breaking the wind, thus reducing the amount of heat pulled from the home. The bitter cold winds of winter can be devastating, as well as bone-chilling. Plant a wind screen far enough from the house that it will allow some air circulation during the summer. Contact your Cooperative Extension office for recommendations for your area.

If you are about to plant a shade tree, don't put it too near the foundation, because the root system will be a problem with drainage or sewer pipes.

Trees can help you stay cool in the summer and warm in the winter; and just think how much energy you will save.

MAIL ORDER
Plants Can't Read

It's too bad plants can't read. Take a look at some of those statements in plant catalogs, such as: "Grows as tall as the house in one season," or "Completely covers 10 square feet in just one year." If only the plants knew what the description in the catalog said they could do — and did it. It would be fantastic.

Since you *can* read, there are several points to consider when using mail order plant and seed catalogs. First, check to see if the firm is a member of the Mailorder Association of Nurserymen. This organization is a self-policing group that helps set standards for its own industry. Another point to look for: are the plants that are advertised hardy in your area? Some catalogs are just for specific growing regions.

Buying plants by mail can save you money, because you are not paying for the shipment of soil, just the roots and shoots. Mail order is another way to find unusual plants that may not be stocked by your local garden center.

What should you expect from your purchase? The size and condition of the plant is important. If the catalog describes it as "well branched and 3-4 feet tall," and you receive a plant that is 1-2 feet tall and has a single stem, send it back. Don't accept plants that do not match the description.

Many mail order houses ship according to zip codes. This allows them to plan shipments into an area according to weather and temperature. If the plants arrive for planting outside, and the ground is frozen, what are you going to do with them? Send them back, or refuse the shipment.

One final caution when ordering by mail. After taking out the order blank, look to see if the address of the company is still printed somewhere in the catalog. There have been instances where, once the order form was removed, the address was gone.

Place your orders as early as possible, so you won't be disappointed by having your order stamped "all sold out."

VEGETABLES

VEGETABLE GARDENING
The Plan of Attack

As discussed in "Landscape Planting," the advice to "plan before you plant" also applies to establishing a vegetable patch. The vegetable garden cannot be thrown together at the last minute. If you try to, it will be a disaster. From the time that the first thought is conceived to the actual planting, a careful step-by-step procedure will assure success.

First, take a family inventory to find out who in your family will eat what. There is no sense growing crops that no one will eat. Growing eggplant, harvesting it, and then watching everyone turn up their noses is no fun. Take the catalogs and have every member of your family select the crops they would enjoy eating. Then, draw up a list and select the best varieties. Each year plan to plant several tried and true varieties, adding a few new selections from the latest introductions. Never plant all newly-introduced varieties. They may not do well in your garden.

Now draw a garden plan. Use the scale of one inch to one foot. Nothing elaborate is needed but the plan will allow for spacing of the crops and give you an idea as to how many plants will fit in a given area. Don't plan to make the entire back yard into a garden. That's too big. Gardens as small as 20x20 feet will yield great quantities of produce, if properly planned. After you have determined the needed size, you may want to increase it by just a few feet to grow a little extra for a friend. There is nothing more rewarding than giving a gift of something you have grown and harvested from your garden.

With the seed list and plan in hand, make out the order for the varieties and amount of seeds you will need. Some catalogs sell seed by weight, generally in fractions of an ounce since most seed is very light in weight. When weight is not a factor some companies will sell seeds by count. Don't order a one-ounce package of broccoli. It contains 3,000 seeds. I doubt if you will need that many of any plant. Crops such as peas, beans, lettuce, radishes, carrots, spinach, and swiss chard are easily started from seed. In addition, you will probably want to purchase some transplants from your garden center when planting time arrives.

VEGETABLE GARDEN IRRIGATION
A Drip at a Time

Every time we need to water the vegetables we get out the sprinkler and soak the whole garden. Great! But each watering of the entire garden wets the walkways. What grows in the walkways? Weeds! To discourage weed growth in the walks, don't water them. Water only the desired plants.

The development of the drip, emitter, or ooze irrigation systems has eliminated unnecessary watering of weeds. There are many systems available for the home garden. Most are Tinkertoy type construction. Just put the parts together and turn on the water. Some have drip tubes or emitters that are inserted into the system at the location of the plant to be watered.

The best way to install the system is to plan the garden on paper first so you know where the plants will be placed. (Example: Tomatoes planted on two-foot centers will have a water outlet at each location.) Install the water system in the garden before you start planting. This way you will not step on the tender new plants. At the end of the season the system can be taken apart and stored over winter for use again next year.

For crops that are grown in tight rows there is the ooze tube system. It is nothing more than a canvas hose that allows water to leak out along the entire row. Watering the garden in this manner will help eliminate the growth of many weeds, and will conserve water as well.

Drip, emitter, and ooze systems can conserve up to 70% of the water usually used when irrigating the garden with overhead sprinklers. Be a good gardener. Conserve one of our most precious resources — water.

MULCHES IN THE VEGETABLE PATCH
Preserve! Destroy! Beautify!

A mulch in the vegetable patch will help conserve precious moisture, keep down pesky weeds, and make the garden aesthetically appealing all summer long. Think of a mulch as nothing but a cover on the surface of the soil. Necessity and economics could determine what is used. It might be the old carpeting from the kitchen, woodchips that the arborist left you when the "old oak" had to come down, black plastic rolled out in the walkways, or the newspaper referred to in "Weeds In the Vegetable Patch."

In many areas moisture is at a premium during the growing season. If anything can be done to conserve it, so much the better. Mulches reduce the amount of evaporation of moisture from the soil and allow rain to penetrate more slowly, thus reducing erosion.

Weeds can germinate without light, but after germination they have to have sufficient light to manufacture food and to grow. So, to kill the weeds, block out light.

For aesthetics, the kitchen carpet might do. The decorative side can be placed facing up. However, if there is a plastic or rubber backing on the carpet, or if it is used as a single piece to cover a large area, small holes should be cut through to allow water to penetrate. The same holds true when using large sheets of black plastic. If either is placed in the walkways only, then it isn't necessary to make holes.

One caution on using black plastic: if fruits, such as melons and squash, are allowed to lie on the plastic, rot may develop at the point of contact. The simple solution is to place a thin bed of straw between the fruit and the black plastic.

WEEDS IN THE VEGETABLE PATCH
The Want Ads?

Countless numbers of gardeners have spent hundreds of hours planning, planting, and caring for their plants only to see the vegetable patch go to weeds. This need not be a problem.

Feeding and watering the desirable plants also makes weeds grow. Hand cultivation to control weeds is a time-consuming task that few gardeners enjoy. Controlling weeds by cultivation means you will be back in a few days doing it again and again and again. Hand cultivation can also damage the roots of the crops you are so carefully nurturing.

There is an inexpensive method of weed control that is available to virtually all gardeners. It's the newspaper. A one-week subscription or a Sunday issue of a major paper should do the job. After the crops are planted and the seeds have started to grow, cultivate the soil to eliminate any weed seeds that have germinated. Then, place sections of newspaper, five layers thick, in the walkways so the ends of the papers overlap a few inches. The newspaper will block out the light needed by the weed seedlings, prohibiting their growth, and the overlapping makes sure that light will not peek between the papers. Don't try four layers. Enough light will penetrate and the weeds will grow. You must use five layers, or more. Do *not* use the color section because of the dyes in the print.

After placing the papers on the soil, wet them. When newspaper gets wet it adheres to the soil better. Scatter grass clippings, wood chips, or soil to anchor the paper for the season.

Caution: Don't put newspapers down on a windy day. You will end up chasing them all over the neighborhood.

"Mommy grows plants in everything."

PROPAGATION CONTAINERS
From the Kitchen

There are many containers available commercially to use in starting seeds. They include peat pots, peat cubes, Jiffy-7's, and miniature greenhouses. They all cost money; they all work; they all can be a good investment for gardening. But, you can save money and accomplish the same results if you use some of the containers we bring home from the grocery store for starting seeds.

Egg cartons are one of my favorites. There are basically two types: paper and styrofoam. The paper cartons work best, though they tend to fall apart from moisture after a period of time. Moisture and air pass through the paper layers, allowing for better root development for the seedlings. There is also less chance of overwatering. With styrofoam cartons you will have to punch several holes in the bottom of each cell to provide proper drainage. Either type of carton can serve as a 12-pack for starting seeds.

The aluminum deli containers with the clear plastic tops are also excellent for starting seeds. These make super little greenhouses. Holes punched in the bottom will allow for proper drainage and air circulation. A well-drained, loose soil mix should be used in the metal containers. The plastic top makes a good cover for the seed germination chamber, because it allows light to penetrate, and it traps humidity. After the seeds begin to grow, remove the cover and water the seedlings according to their needs. Start only one variety per container. Be sure to label each one with the variety name and the date planted.

TOMATOES
Reflections

Tomatoes need as much light as possible in order to grow and produce fruit. If there is inadequate light, the plants will develop spindly growth and will not produce flowers and fruit. Not everyone who would like to grow tomatoes has a totally sunny environment, but you can overcome that handicap in the following ways:

Light can be reflected to the plants. If you plant the tomatoes next to a white wall, there will be a considerable increase in the amount of light that the plants receive. If the plant receives a half day of direct sun and reflected light from the white wall for the balance of the day, the tomatoes will produce.

Another method of reflecting light is to use strips of 18" wide aluminum foil. Place the foil, shiny side up, on the surface of the soil under the plant. The light will strike the foil and help light up the foliage. However, do not put the foil under the plant until the soil warms sufficiently for the roots to develop properly.

An added benefit from the foil is pest control. When the light is reflected to the bottom side of the leaves the pests, such as aphids and mites, which love the shade, will crawl to the top side of the leaf, but the sun is up there. After two or three trips around the leaf, the pests will give up and go to your neighbors. The benefit of aluminum foil is reduced when the plants grow large enough to shade themselves.

TOMATOES
Crutches or Cages?

Training your favorite pet is not easy, but it makes it a better citizen. Similarly, training your tomato plants takes time, but it will result in less sun scald, cracking, and decay, and you will have even fewer problems with slugs — just exactly the results you want. There is no other crop in the vegetable patch that will benefit more from such a little effort.

The training that is necessary depends on the type of plant you select. Determinate varieties are bush-type and generally do not exceed three feet in height. Indeterminate varieties are tall-growing and definitely need staking or caging.

If you use a stake as the support, place it in the ground before planting the tomato to avoid damaging the roots. The plant will eventually become heavy as it matures and produces fruit, so select a stake that is strong enough not to break in a wind. Tie the plant to the stake, but do not use wire or string. They will cut the stem. Instead, use strips of cloth, or nylon from worn out nylon stockings. Do not tie the stem tight to the pole.

Tomato cages are good, because no tying is necessary and they support the plant as it grows. However, care should be taken in selecting cages. Many are so flimsy they will collapse in the wind or from the eventual load of the plant. You can make a very strong cage from #12 reinforcing wire (6"x6" openings). Do not make a cage from chicken wire, since the holes are only two inches square and you will not be able to get your hands in to do the harvesting. Besides, you can't pull a five-inch tomato through a one-inch hole!

The neatest system I have ever used calls for a horizontal support. It is constructed of four-foot wide #12 reinforcing wire supported two feet off the ground with legs at six-foot intervals made of 2x4s. The plants can be guided up through the wire until they spread out to provide their own shade. All the fruit hangs underneath and is easy to reach. Once it's erected — no slugs, no sun scald, no cracking, and no work.

TOMATOES
The Biggest on the Block

Want the biggest tomatoes on the block? There are several cultural practices that just may enable you to produce them. In order to grow the biggest fruits you must start with the right plant. Don't expect two-to-three-pound tomatoes on varieties like Tiny Tim or cherry. It just won't happen, no matter what you do. Select plants that have the capability of producing big tomatoes.

Plant them properly. They need full sun, well-drained soil, nutrients such as 5-10-10 plus the trace elements, and water during dry periods.

The secret in developing a strong plant to produce the largest fruit is a procedure that will wipe you out psychologically. When the first sets of flowers begin to form, pinch them off. This will allow the plant to become better established before going into the fruiting cycle. If the plant is allowed to become better rooted in the early part of the season, it will be able to produce more prolifically during the hot, dry weather.

The second secret: when the next sets of flowers form, let them complete setting fruit. But when the tomatoes are about the size of your little fingernail pinch all but two out of the cluster. (You will notice that tomato plants often produce three to five tomatoes in a cluster.) Continue to do this to all of the fruiting clusters as the season progresses. You will have groups of two all over the plant. The reason for this is to concentrate all the energy into the production of fewer but better fruits.

A little tip: If this is the first time that you are trying this, do it to only half of your plants. You will not become as mentally disturbed. I guarantee you will do it to all of your tomato plants next year.

THE CUCURBIT FAMILY
You Be the Bee

The cucurbit family includes squash, melons, and cucumbers. Each year these are planted after the last frost date, with great expectations of picking hundreds of fruits, but it does not always happen. The plants start to grow, they are fed regularly, and flowers begin to blossom, but no fruit sets. There are several reasons for the fruitless plants. Let's look at two of them.

The curcurbit family produces both male and female blossoms on the same plant. The male blossoms are produced on a long, pencil-like petiole, and the female blossoms on a very short petiole. It is not unusual for the plant to start its flowering cycle with male blossoms. If this is the case, be patient. The plant will eventually produce the female counterpart. Just continue feeding and watering as needed.

Another reason for lack of fruit set is lack of pollination. The male blossom opens in the morning when there is often 70% to 80% humidity. During this time the bee activity may be minimal, so there are fewer carriers of pollen. The female blossom opens around noon. If the bees have not visited the male blossoms in the morning they will have no pollen to carry to the female. The solution: In the morning collect several of the male blossoms that are wide open. These are the ones that are ready to release their pollen. Lay them on a paper and take them inside until early afternoon. Then take them back out to the garden, peel the flower petals back to expose the pollen in the male blossom, and "dingle" it over the female flowers. You be the bee!

WIDE-ROW PLANTING AND BLOCK PLANTING
36 Feet of Lettuce?

In America vegetable gardens are usually laid out in nice, neat, straight rows with walkways that are wide enough to drive a truck through. In order to make the garden more productive, and have fewer walkways for the weeds to grow in, why not try block planting or wide-row planting? With a proper design you can eliminate many of the walks and increase the production per square foot. In fact, you will be able to grow the same quantity of vegetables in a much smaller area.

To plan the wide-row garden, inventory the crops you plan to grow. Some of them may be grown in double or triple rows planted close together. Using the wide-row concept, plants such as bush beans, broccoli, peas, or spinach can be planted in two or three rows spaced 10 to 12 inches apart.

Block planting is the growing of rows four feet wide and as long as you wish. Remember, you want to be able to reach the middle of the block, so don't make it wider than you can comfortably stretch to harvest the crop.

If you plant lettuce in a long, straight row in your garden you will probably become over-zealous and plant more than you can eat at any one time. All of the lettuce will mature at the same time and I defy any family to eat 36 feet of lettuce in one week. In contrast to this, use one type of block planting for your lettuce. Plant two rows, four feet long, across the block, the first week; then two more rows the next week, and so on. You will have lettuce maturing in eatable succession, eight feet at a time.

Other crops that enjoy block planting are cabbage, onions, garlic, and radishes. Cabbage should be planted on 12-inch centers. Onions and garlic may be as close as four inches to each other. Radish rows in the block should be spaced no further apart than the span of a hand.

Try wide-row or block planting. Either will eliminate many weeds, because there will be fewer walks, and the plants will begin to grow together to block out light to the weeds.

"Remove the covers in the morning."

THE VEGETABLE PATCH
Bedsheets and Bushel Baskets

In regions where frost ends the gardening season prematurely, there are ways to extend the harvesting period. It is very depressing to see plants produce fruit and not be able to harvest them because they have been hit by frost. Often we have a killing frost, only to have it followed by several weeks of Indian summer weather. If our plants could make it through the first frost, they could continue to grow and produce fruit.

To help extend the harvest, pay attention to the weatherman. Be ready to act quickly when the frost warning comes. For light frost protection, place bed sheets over the plants in the evening to trap heat around them. Bushel baskets placed over small plants will accomplish the same thing. Remove the covers in the morning and let in the sunshine.

Turning on the overhead sprinkler in the early morning, before sunup, can also prevent frost damage. The water helps raise the temperature immediately around the plant. It can be turned off after sunrise.

If protection is not possible for your tomatoes, pick them all the night before the frost. Examine each fruit for cracks and blemishes. Fruits that are in excellent condition can be wrapped individually in single layers of newspaper and stored, with the stem end down, in a dark, cool basement. Cool temperatures and the lack of light will slow the ripening process. As you want the tomatoes to ripen, unwrap them, keep them at room temperature (not in the sun because they will lose their vitamin content), and they will be ready to eat in just a few days. Don't forget — you must get there before Jack Frost does.

INDOOR VEGETABLE PATCH
Your Own Salad

If you don't have an area outdoors in which you can grow vegetables, you can grow them indoors. Imagine harvesting tomatoes, green peppers, lettuce, and cucumbers from your indoor vegetable patch.

There are some cultural practices that must be adhered to. First, you must have a bright, sunny window for crops that produce fruit. The container must be large enough to support the size of the plant and to accommodate the roots as they develop. Regular feeding and watering are necessary. Varieties must be those that are bush or patio size. There are many to select from.

The trick to getting fruit set indoors is pollination. Outside you have the bees and the wind to do the pollinating for you. Indoors, you have to be the bee. As the flowers on the tomatoes and eggplants begin to open, you must trigger the pollen. Simply tap the blossom with your finger and a puff of pollen will be released to complete pollination. For cucumbers one additional problem exists. They have both male and female flowers. The male is on a long, pencil-like petiole and the female is on a very short petiole. Without wind or bee activity there is no natural way of cross pollination. Simply pick off a male blossom that is wide open and "dingle" it over an open female blossom. You have now pollinated the female flower, and fruit can set. You have been the bee.

Lettuce in a window box is quite easy to grow, and it can be grown in a little less sunlight than that needed for fruiting plants. Select leafy varieties that mature in a short time. Keep watering and feeding as recommended for the variety you are growing.

It won't be long before you will have the lettuce, tomatoes, peppers, and cucumbers for your salad.

GENERAL
HORTICULTURE

WINDOW BOXES
A Headache? Or a Pleasure?

First, the window box can become a headache if it is not properly attached to the window sill. It must be anchored so wind and rain do not cause it to fall. In some areas there are local laws and/or building code regulations that prohibit the use of window boxes above the first floor. Check with the building inspector before installation.

Secondly, planting in window boxes can be a problem because most do not have drainage holes. Without drains, rain can fill the container and drown the plants. To lessen the drainage problem place a layer of coarse gravel in the bottom of the box. To provide additional protection for the plants, you can double pot. Grow the plants in clay pots, set them in the window box, and fill in between the pots with a lightweight mix. If you suspect the container is getting too much water, lift out one of the pots and look. If one plant becomes a problem it can easily be replaced without disturbing the other plants.

On the other hand, a window box can be an excellent area for growing plants. During the summer annuals can provide color and in the winter evergreen branches can be placed there.

Plant the annuals in a well-draining potting mix. Use one part soil, one part peat moss, and two parts perlite. Do not use sand, because of its weight.

Feeding plants in window boxes is the same as with any other plants. For flowers use a low-nitrogen fertilizer, such as 5-10-5, and for foliage plants, use a high-nitrogen food, such as 12-6-6, or their equivalents.

VEGETABLE GARDENING IN CONTAINERS
A Conversation Piece

Growing vegetables on the terrace or patio can be a conversation piece when company comes, but also it can be productive. For example, in a sunny area, you can grow potatoes, tomatoes, pole beans, and peppers.

Potatoes can be grown in a pillow sack — a large plastic pillowcase that is filled with a growing media and sealed on both ends. Small slits are made on the upper side of the pillow, and the potato eyes, or seedlings, are planted in through the holes. Watering and feeding are easy. Just pour water, mixed with fertilizer, into the holes. In mid-season, reach into the mix and steal a few small potatoes. They're really tasty.

Tomatoes are best grown in large containers in a well-drained media, using one part soil, one part peat moss, and one part perlite, mixed together. Feed with a water-soluble fertilizer, such as 15-30-15 or equivalent. Select short, bushy varieties unless you have a trellis to attach them to. Cherry tomatoes can be grown in hanging baskets.

Pole beans grow well on a "teepee" support. Use three large containers, placing them at the three points of a triangle, about 18 inches apart. Using six-foot-long bamboo poles as the trellis, push the base of one pole into each container filled with the growing media. The same formula of mix you used for the tomatoes is fine. Bend the tops of the poles so they all touch, and then tie them together. Plant four beans per pot. Water and feed them as recommended for tomatoes. The beans will climb the trellis and begin producing in no time at all.

A beautiful, compact plant for the patio was just introduced in 1983 by the Park Seed Co., Greenwood, South Carolina — it's the Thai hot pepper. However, if you have friends or children who love to help themselves, don't let them pick one of these peppers. Italian hot peppers are mild, compared to the Thai hot pepper.

SOIL TESTING
A Teaspoonful?

Soil testing is nothing more than an inventory of what is in the soil at the time the sample is taken. Testing a sample can tell you the pH (soil acidity), nutrient and organic content, and drainage capabilities. Not all of the above needs to be done for the average garden or lawn.

Soils vary greatly from one side of the property to the other. In fact, the soil can vary from one foot to the next. That is why we recommend that soil averaging be done. Samples may be taken from several areas and mixed together for an average reading. If there are specific gardens or areas growing one specific crop, such as the lawn, these samples should be held separate. Why? The treatment for the lawn will most likely be different from the treatment for the vegetable or flower garden.

Take several random samples of soil to a depth of at least six inches. This will give a soil profile in the area where the roots are to grow. The sample submitted must be sufficient. Usually, most soils labs require a minimum of four cups for testing. Don't take them a teaspoonful and ask them to test your soil.

If the soil pH is tested, the results will tell you if you need lime or sulfur. There is no reason to add either if it is not needed.

Nutrient tests can be quite complex. In most cases the nitrogen, phosphorus, and potassium are the elements that are tested. These are the major elements needed for plant growth. If you suspect that the trace elements, such as boron, magnesium, zinc, etc., are missing, you will need to request a trace element test. I recommend this test to many gardeners who have been using the same plot over and over. Certain crops, grown year after year in the same spot, can deplete the soil of certain elements. If the soil is missing the element the crop may do poorly. (Example: A test may identify the need for one teaspoon of boron per acre to correct the deficiency. Apply it.)

Generally, tests are not needed for organic content. Each year simply add the decomposed material from the compost pile.

Drainage can be tested in the garden. Dig a hole and fill it with water. If the water has drained completely in 24 hours, most plants will do well.

Gardeners, test your soil!

TESTING SEEDS
A Seed Saver

Every year when ordering seeds, we end up with more than we can possibly use. Sharing them with the neighbors could be a solution, but they may not want to grow the same plants. Don't throw the seeds out; save them.

By keeping the seeds in their original packets, and sealing them up tight, we have both saved the planting information, and shut out light that might do harm. Place the packages in jars that can be tightly sealed, to eliminate outside moisture, and store them in a cool, dark place. Next year we have some seeds to get the garden started — or do we? Before celebrating the accomplishment, test the seeds to see if they have survived the storage months.

Some seeds lose their viability in a short time. Count out ten seeds and place them on a damp paper towel. Roll up the towel, place it in a plastic bag, seal it tight, label it with the variety and date, and store the sample in a warm area — 70-75 degrees is sufficient. Read the back of the seed packet for the germination time of your seeds. If it says 10 days, wait that amount of time before you open the bag and roll out the paper towel. Count the number of seeds that have a little thread-like growth coming from one end. (This is the root beginning to show.) If six of the ten seeds have growth there is 60% germination. It is at this point that the decision is made whether new seeds must be ordered.

By the way, careful ordering will help eliminate the need for seed storage. One ounce of broccoli seed doesn't sound like a lot until you realize that one ounce contains about 3,000 seeds. You can't grow that many plants in a lifetime, even if you could save the seeds that long.

PROPAGATING SEEDS
A Complete Collapse?

Starting and growing seedlings can be quite an experience. After you have started your own, you definitely will learn to respect the commercial grower. You sow the seeds, water them to start germination, watch them begin to grow — only to see them fold over and die. This problem is known as "damping-off" disease. It is caused by several soil fungi, some of which can cause the germinating seeds to die before they even emerge.

There are several poor cultural practices that encourage damping-off. They include: dirty pots, nonsterilized soil, too much moisture, humid conditions, stagnant air around the seedlings, and even dirty hands.

To help prevent damping-off, start with a sterilized propagating mix in a clean, well-drained container. Always seed in rows rather than broadcasting over the surface, because if damping-off starts, it can wipe out an entire flat of seeds in one night. Row planting impedes the spread of the organism.

Place the mix in the container and make slight impressions for your rows of seeds. In each shallow trench sprinkle milled sphagnum moss. On the bed of moss sow the seeds and then cover the seeds with another thin layer of sphagnum moss. The moss has an antiseptic quality and will prohibit the damping-off organism. Fungicides are available to help provide additional protection.

Start one variety of seed in each container. Otherwise, the different germination time for different kinds of plants makes seedling management in a container difficult.

When the seeds begin to emerge, provide quality light and air circulation, and begin to reduce the moisture.

Water seedlings early in the day, never just before dark unless they show wilting signs. Seedlings that go into night in an overly moist condition are candidates for damping-off.

THE COMPOST PILE
A Gardener's "Black Gold"

The price of gold is on the increase, along with the price of oil. The cost of a bale of peat moss is going up too, but you can save your money by making the gardener's "black gold" right in your own back yard.

Decomposed plant material is the best source of organic matter that is available. It is valuable to the soil because it is basically humic acid, the cement which holds soil together as well as apart.

The construction of a compost pile can be as simple or as complex as you want to make it. The end result will be the same. Find a place in the garden that is exposed to the natural elements of sun and rain. Using a shovel, dish out an area so water will collect in it when it rains. Save the soil that is removed, piling it over to one side. The first layer of organic matter can be grass clippings, cabbage leaves, leaves from the trees, etc. Make the layer about one foot thick, but be sure to make the layer dished in the center. This will allow the pile to catch rainfall. Take two shovels of garden soil (the soil you saved at the beginning), and sprinkle it over the first layer of organic matter. This soil is loaded with bacteria which will inoculate the organic matter and initiate decomposition. Continue adding new layers of organic matter, along with the sprinkling of soil. Remember to leave it dished in the center. If it has not rained before you add each new layer, wet the pile down thoroughly. Water is required, plus bacteria, in order to make the organic matter into humic acid, the product that is so valuable to your soil.

I never add lime or fertilizer to my pile, because I never know exactly where I will use the compost. I don't turn the pile, either. The center is completely broken down to a "black gold" liquid by spring, and the outer shell, of partially decomposed material, is the beginning of next year's compost.

Why not make your own "black gold?" It's worth it.

"Do I need all of this for my garden?"

SOIL AMENDMENTS
A Silk Purse Out of a Sow's Ear?

Contrary to the old saying, the gardener *can* make a silk purse out of a sow's ear. That's exactly what we do when we incorporate soil amendments or additives into a poor soil to make it useful and productive. Such soil amendments can include lime, sulfur, gypsum, peat moss, compost, fertilizer, sand, etc., depending upon the deficiencies. (See "Soil Testing")

Lime and sulfur are used to adjust the pH of the soil. If the soil is too acid, lime is applied to make it more alkaline. If the soil is too alkaline, sulfur is added to create an acid condition.

Gypsum and sand are incorporated into the soil to improve aeration and drainage. Gypsum (calcium sulfate) is slow-acting, but it will open heavy clay soils to make them more porous. Sand creates bulk and provides channels, or tiny pockets, for holding air, as well as allowing the passage of water.

Peat moss and compost are excellent sources of organic matter. As organic matter decomposes, humic acid is formed which is the "cement" that holds soil particles together as well as apart. Decomposed organic matter in the soil also improves the nutrient-holding capacity, although the organic materials themselves are not nutrients.

Fertilizer, added in proper proportions, will supply the nutrients needed for growth. Remember, there are many formulas for fertilizers. Select the one best suited for the plant being grown.

Adding soil amendments is like baking a cake. You must mix the ingredients thoroughly before they will produce the desired results, and they must be added in proper proportions.

FORCING BLOOMS INDOORS
I Just Can't Wait!

Every February I start to get the wintertime blues. I want to see spring flowers, even though I know none will start blooming for several weeks. That's when I get out the pruning shears and prune my outdoor plants — some of them, that is. I will bring some branches indoors and force them into bloom.

Apple, pear, peach, forsythia, lilac, and witch hazel are just a few of the plants that can provide you with a late-winter boost and an early peek at what normally would be spring blossoms.

Cut off branches that were produced last year, because they are the stems that contain the flowering mechanisms for the coming year. Using a hammer, smash the lower part of the stem and place it in a container of warm water. Set the container in moderate light (no full sun), and, in a few days, the buds will begin to pop. Keep fresh water in the container, and soon you will have blossoms in your home.

If you prune the plants carefully, they will not miss the branches you have removed; in fact, this could become part of your regular, early-spring pruning ritual.

FORCING BULBS
The Refrigerator

Many spring flowering bulbs can be grown indoors to provide fragrance and beauty. The technique is called "forcing." Crocuses, grape-hyacinths, hyacinths, narcissuses, and tulips are excellent candidates. However, unless the bulb is marked "precooled" or "ready for forcing" there is one step that must be taken before the bulb will produce its flower. The bulb must be cooled in order to trigger the flowering mechanism.

Bulbs can be cool treated in two basic ways. *One:* In the late fall, pot the bulbs in a standard bulb pan. Dig a trench in the garden, place the potted bulbs in the trench, and cover them with a mix containing coarse sand. The winter freezing action will provide refrigeration for the bulbs. Allow at least six weeks to elapse at temperatures no warmer than 40 degrees. The bulbs, in their container, can then be taken from the sand mix and brought to room temperature. Do not place the bulbs in full sun; the new shoots, having inadequate chlorophyll, will burn. After the green begins to show, the container can be placed in a cool, sunny window and watered regularly. They will bloom shortly.

Two: In areas where the temperature does not drop enough to provide the necessary cooling, use the refrigerator. Pot the bulbs and moisten the soil. Slip the container into a paper bag and place it in the hydrator or lettuce crisper, where it is usually about 40 degrees. After six weeks the bulbs may be removed and forced as stated above. With the refrigerator method, be sure to label the pot so the family doesn't eat the bulbs.

CUT FLOWERS
Love 'em Longer

A beautiful way to brighten your home environment, at any time of the year, is to purchase a cut-flower arrangement from your florist; or, make your own arrangement from flowers you have grown or purchased. The beauty and fresh appearance of your bouquet can be extended with some consideration and a little action on your part.

If you are purchasing flowers, buy them from a reputable shop. Be sure they are using fresh flowers and not those left over from last week. You will often receive a small packet of flower life-extender with your purchase. Use it.

For cut flowers, always start with a clean container. Wash the vase with hot, soapy water to remove any bacteria that may cling to the inside. Fill it with fresh, lukewarm water. Make a fresh cut, one inch up from the base of the stem, and remove any of the lower foliage that would be in the water. Foliage that is placed in water will decay quickly, reducing the life of the flowers. Add fresh water daily, and make a new cut, again one inch up from the base of the stem. This procedure allows for the continual uptake of water by the flower.

Do not place cut flowers, or a flower arrangement, in the direct sun. Without roots, they cannot take up enough water fast enough to survive.

Keep cut flowers as cool as possible. At night you can even put them in the refrigerator, but remove any apples that might be stored in the hydrator. The ethylene gas given off by the apples will put your flowers to sleep.

PRESSING PLANTS
The Yellow Pages

Many beautiful and creative pictures can be made from flowers and foliage that have been preserved by pressing. It is a simple task if you take the phone book into the garden when you start picking. You need to press most plants immediately, especially the leaves. The phone book is preferred, because it has soft, absorbent paper.

On each page spread out a leaf. Note the page and mark its number in your records so you will know that, for instance, on page 66 is a tiny maple leaf. Otherwise, it might be hard to find the little rascal later when you want him. Separate each specimen with several pages. This will ensure that the leaves will not leave an imprint on each other, and the moisture from one will not affect the other. At the end of each day of collecting, close the book and place a stack of several heavy books on top of it to act as a press. Care should be taken to provide warmth for drying and good air circulation around the stack.

A project that can be enjoyed by the whole family is making place mats for the kitchen table from your pressed collections. Cut adhesive shelf paper into a 12-inch by 18-inch rectangle. Lay the paper sticky side up, and arrange the leaves and flowers in an attractive pattern. The names of the plants can be typed on cards and inserted next to the leaves. Cover the montage with clear plastic, and trim the edges.

Caution: leaves that are placed on the sticky side of the paper can only be put down once, so plan your pattern *first*.

From the beginning of the growing season, start collecting foliage to obtain different stages of growth, from the very newest leaves to the ones Mother Nature paints in the fall with the brilliant yellows, reds, and oranges.

DRYING WILD FLOWERS
Know the Law

Gaining in popularity over the past few years, dried flowers are found in virtually every flower and gift shop in the world. Perhaps this is because the flower arrangements made from them don't need to be fed or watered.

Collecting flowers from the wild should begin in the spring and continue through late fall, even after the frost, but there are several cautions that must be adhered to.

First, learn to identify those plants which are on the endangered list; of course, you do not want to pick any of these. Second, pick only one or two flowers from any one area; this will insure that Mother Nature can replenish the supply next year. And third, *before* you pick, always ask permission of the owner of the property on which the plant is growing.

There are many wild flowers that will enhance an arrangement: cattails, goldenrod, wild carrot top, wild daisy, etc.

To dry cattails and goldenrod, remove all the foliage so only the flower stalk remains. (The foliage would just wither and fall apart.) Tie several stems in a bunch and hang them in a warm, dark closet or attic. After a few weeks, the flowers and stems will be dry. To prevent the cattail head from shattering, spray it with a generous portion of hair spray. Use the spray for hard-to-hold hair. Goldenrod can also be sprayed to reduce shattering of its delicate yellow flowers.

For wild carrot and daisy, pinch off the head and dry it in silica gel, or another drying preparation. The stems can be air-dried and later the flowers can be reattached with a toothpick and glue by pushing one end of a sticky pick into the hollow stem and inserting the other end into the base of the flower.

You will enjoy collecting, drying, and using plants from the wild.

DRIED FLOWERS FROM THE GARDEN
Three-Dimensional

The flower garden is the place to find many candidates for dried flower arrangements. Marigolds, zinnias, chrysanthemums, roses, hydrangeas, salvias, and flowering onions are just a few. Two methods for drying flowers are to hang them upside down in a warm, dark area, or, to place them in a drying medium.

Hanging is simple. Remove any foliage, tie the stems in bunches, and hang them upside down. The foliage must be removed, because it will only wither and become entangled; then it will drop off and make a mess.

Media drying entails a little more effort. Silica gel, sold commercially, or a mixture of one part white cornmeal and one part borax, will allow for rapid drying of the flower heads. Use white cornmeal, not yellow, because yellow cornmeal will discolor the flowers.

Pour a one-inch layer of the drying media in a moisture-tight container. Press the flower heads gently, stem first, into the mixture. Then, evenly sprinkle the media over the flower head until it is completely covered. Close the container to keep out any additional moisture, and wait for 10 to 14 days. After this period of time, gently pour off the media and you will find a beautiful, but dusty, flower. Use a sable artist's brush to remove the excess media.

Flowers suitable for drying by this method include roses, marigolds, chrysanthemums, zinnias, salvias, and amaranthas. If stems are needed, air dry the stems by hanging.

When using dried arrangements, do not place them in the direct sun. The color will bleach out and the flowers will eventually turn brown.

PESTS

IPM
No, It's Not a Computer Company!

Integrated Pest Management (IPM) is a term that will be heard more and more in years to come. With today's technology and advances in agriculture, pest control has become easier than ever. There is a spray for just about every problem or pest in the garden. But before you decide to spray for everything, think twice. IPM is a philosophy which includes selecting resistant plant varieties and practicing sanitation, as well as using biological, mechanical, and chemical controls. Singly, or in combination, these methods will eliminate many pest problems.

Plant breeders are developing new plant varieties that are resistant to diseases and insects.

Sanitation includes cleaning the garden, keeping weeds down which make good homes for pests, and roguing out sick plants.

Biological controls are natural controls found in the environment. They include predators and parasites, as well as induced diseases that live on the "bad guys." Example: controlling the Japanese beetle grub by the use of milky spore disease; releasing sterilized, male adults to control the Mediterranean fruit fly.

Mechanical controls include traps to catch the adults. The gypsy moth trap lures the male moth, and the Japanese beetle trap attracts both the male and female adult. The old sticky flypaper is another mechanical method.

You will find some traps that work and some that don't. Before you invest, do a little research to see if they really work. Some ads falsely lead you to believe that their product is God's gift to the world of pest control.

Pesticides are the last line of defense in the IPM system. However, no matter what pesticide you choose, *read the label and follow the manufacturer's recommended rates and directions.* By using IPM you will use far fewer pesticides.

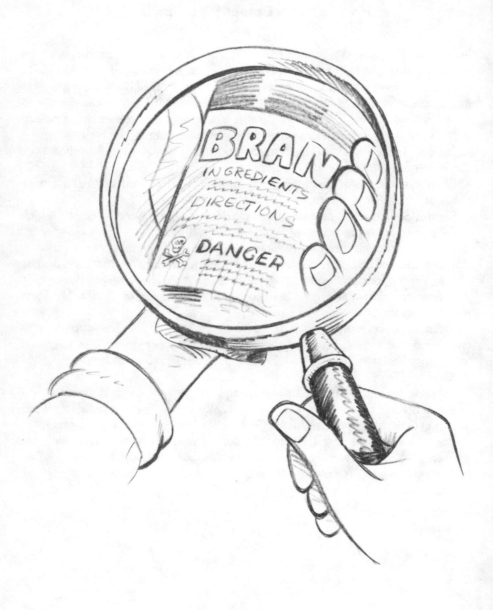

PESTICIDES
Read the Label

Any time you use a pesticide, whether it is an insecticide, miticide, herbicide, or fungicide, follow the cardinal rule of gardening: *Read the label.* Never trust your memory regarding rate of application, mixing instructions, or even the crop clearance. The label of a particular pesticide may change from year to year. The pesticide you used last year may be formulated differently now. The manufacturer has spent hundreds of thousands of dollars figuring out how his product works best. "If one ounce will do it, two will do it better" is *not* true; so *read the label.*

The information on the label is important. Read it carefully, and understand the directions. Keep good records of the pesticides you use and what they are applied to. Information to be kept in the garden diary includes: the manufacturer's name, the name of the product, the active ingredient, the rate of application, and what crop it was applied to. With this information you can seek help if there should be a problem.

Pay careful attention to crop clearance: pesticides are registered and formulated to control specific problems with specific crops, and this must be indicated on the label.

Cleanup and disposal are also pertinent. There are specific instructions on the label that tell you how to dispose of the empty container, and how to clean your equipment. *Never* pour extra pesticides on the ground. *Read the label.*

Cautions: Read the hazards and the environmental statement. This paragraph, found on every label, may frighten you. This shouldn't prevent you from using a pesticide where it is needed, but perhaps you will be more mindful of indiscriminate use, as opposed to potential benefit from the use of these products. *Read the label and follow the manufacturer's recommended rates and directions.*

APHIDS
Loved by Ladybugs

The aphid is probably among the pests that you as a gardener are most familiar with. Aphids are tiny plant lice, about 1/16 of an inch long, that pierce and suck the life from the plant. They come in green, yellow, red, brown, purple, and white. When they are feeding, they secrete a liquid as their waste that hosts a fungus called sooty mold. Left unchecked, the aphid will produce several generations in one growing season. Aphids love roses, petunias, salvias, tomatoes, peppers, cabbages, lettuce, etc. The young tender growth is its favorite location.

Biological controls for the aphid are found in nature. A ladybug can devour many aphids in one day, so encourage the friendly insect to live in your garden. If you want to purchase ladybugs, you can order them by mail, but order no more than a matchbox full — that is 500 ladybugs. Don't order a gallon — that may be as many as 30,000. You won't need that many.

Don't release newly-arrived ladybugs in the daytime. When the package arrives, put it in the refrigerator until night. The package will be completely closed leaving the ladybugs in the dark. If you were to release them in the sunlight, they would become confused and scatter to the wind. You want them to settle on your property. Let them out after the sun goes down.

Aphids can be controlled with the proper use of pesticides, if the directions are followed. Caution on using pesticides: if you are also trying to use ladybugs as a biological control, you must use pesticides that do not affect the ladybugs.

MITES AND SPIDER MITES
Dust? Or Dandruff?

Many of our plants, both indoors and out, are susceptible to a tiny "critter" which can escape detection until its population explodes. This pest is the mite. Both the common mite and the spider mite can damage foliage and flowers. Symptoms of their work include discolored or bleached leaves, a stippled appearance in the leaves, and the failure of flower buds to open. Mites come in red, green, yellow and brown. Each female is capable of laying up to 100 eggs during its life cycle. Mites pierce and suck the life right out of a plant. The stippled look results from actual removal or destruction of the chlorophyll in the cells.

To test for mites, hold a piece of white paper under a suspect leaf and tap the leaf vigorously. Dust will fall on the paper. Look closely. If the "dust" moves, it's mites. Another way to test is to press a piece of clear sticky tape to the bottom side of a leaf. Again, examine closely the "dust" that adheres to the tape (perhaps with a magnifying glass). If you find tiny six or eight-legged critters, they are mites.

For spider mites, of which there are several species, examine the plant for webbing. Tiny webs may occur at the base of the leaves or at the point where the leaves are attached to the stem. The new growing tips may appear to be wrapped in webs. This is most likely the work of the spider mite.

To control mites, both indoors and outdoors, there are recommended miticides. *Read the label.* A new treatment recommended for mites is insecticidal soap. Several applications may be necessary, no matter what you use. Washing plants and pots will also help control mites. Remember, sanitation is part of IPM (Integrated Pest Management).

MEALYBUGS
Little Cotton Balls

Have you noticed a sticky substance on the table underneath some of your plants, or a black, sticky film on the topside of the leaves? It could be that mealybugs are multiplying. The sticky liquid is a dead giveaway of something piercing and sucking the life out of the plants.

Mother mealybug deposits 300 to 600 eggs in a cottony mass on the leaves, stems, and trunks of the plants. The eggs hatch in 6 to 20 days. That is why the population mushrooms so quickly. Mother can also give birth to live babies. There are many species of mealybugs, and hardly a plant that they don't attack. Outdoors they love yews, pines, citrus, azaleas, etc. Indoors they go after ficus, jades, coleus, impatiens, begonias, cactuses, philodendrons, ivies, etc.

It takes persistence to control mealybugs. Washing plants will help remove mother and the egg masses. The problem is, they get into the cracks and crevices of the foliage, stems, and buds. It is virtually impossible to wash in all these places.

The use of pesticides is another approach. There is a new pesticide, insecticidal soap, that with several applications, according to the label directions, provides control. Do a thorough job when washing and spraying to make sure you clean and spray into all parts of the plant.

For plants such as African violets that have pubescence (tiny little hairs) on the foliage, a cotton swab dipped into a nicotine solution will help. Cook one cigarette (any brand) in two tablespoonfuls of water to leach out the nicotine. After it cools, you can dip the cotton swab into the mixture and then wipe the mealybugs and egg masses off the plant. The solution left on the leaf will provide some residual control. When any remaining bugs walk through the residue, you have them.

"It can't be snow in July!"

WHITEFLY
Snow on the Crop?

Brushing against a plant, either indoors or outside, and seeing a cloud of white, flying insects rise around the plant is a sure indicator of the pest, whitefly. They love to pierce and suck the life out of many of our house and garden plants, such as annuals, perennials, and vegetables including tomatoes, peppers, squash, pumpkins, cucumbers, and eggplants. There are many other susceptible plants, too.

In the vegetable or flower garden, control starts with the recognition of the arrival of the problem. Attach a bright yellow piece of plastic to a stake so it is positioned about two feet off the ground. Coat the plastic with an oil or grease. When the whitefly begin to emerge in the garden, they will be attracted to the yellow and get stuck on the grease or oil. Observe the trap several times a week at the beginning of mid-summer, which is the time that they can begin to mushroom in population. Apply the proper control. There are several commercial pesticides that will alleviate the problem. Also, sanitation is essential in the garden. Keep tall weeds down, as this is where the whitefly develop and overwinter.

Whitefly in the home can be controlled with insecticides, too. *Read the label*. A trick that is also effective is the use of the vacuum cleaner. Place two mothballs in the canister or dust bag and attach the hose to the vacuum cleaner. Touch the plant and turn on the motor. When the adult whiteflies rise, suck them up into the vacuum. Do this every three or four days for at least one month. But don't forget to put the mothballs in the dustbag or canister to kill the whitefly, or in just a few weeks, you will have the darndest case of "critters" incubating in the vacuum.

SCALE
Warts on the Plant

Many plants develop little bumps on their leaves, stems, and trunks. They may look like warts. The bump may turn out to be part of the plant, or it could be a pest called scale. To find out which it is try to lightly scrape the bump off the plant tissue. If it is removed with little pressure, it is most likely scale. Another tell-tale sign is a sticky residue on the surface of the leaves below the affected area.

There are many species of scale. They appear as cottony, cushion-like masses, crusty welts, somewhat flattened, in red, brown, gray, or white. Scale pierce and suck the life out of the plant. A severe infestation can cause defoliation of the entire plant.

Scale attack plants both indoors and outdoors. They love citruses, gardenias, spider plants, scheffleras, ficuses, etc. Outside they work on flowering cherry, hemlock, lilac, peach, pine, etc.

To control scale on houseplants, start with sanitation. Give the plant a bath. Clean off as many of the wart-like scale as possible. Then apply insecticidal soap or other pesticide, thoroughly spraying the plant. Care should be taken to spray into all cracks and crevices where the scale hide. After cleaning the plant and applying the pesticide, mark a spot on a leaf or stem and reexamine the plant in two or three weeks. Then, if this area is clear, it will be your check for success.

Landscape plants can be sprayed with dormant oil before the new growth begins in the spring. Read the label for precautions on temperature and species. Some plants are sensitive to the dormant oils.

SLUGS
Ooey, Gooey!

What "critter" is slippery, slimy, has as many as 100 rows of teeth with up to 90 teeth per row, and loves to eat just about anything in the garden, including marigolds, petunias, begonias, roses, lettuce, cabbage, strawberries, broccoli, Brussels sprouts, tomatoes, salvia, phlox, kale, asparagus, geraniums, chrysanthemums, melons, squash, cucumbers, daisies, zinnias, astilbe, impatiens, collards, beet tops, and peppers (just to name a few)? It's a slug!

Slugs are members of the same family as escargot, clams, and oysters, but they are *not* edible. For its size, the slug is one of the most destructive pests in the vegetable or flower garden.

Slugs eat at night and hide in damp, cool locations during the day. You will know if slugs have visited, not only by the missing parts of plants, but by their slimy trail left on the leaves, walks, and driveway surfaces. Several generations are produced in one season, and one egg mass, which looks like caviar or fish eggs, produces as many as 100 hungry critters.

Slug baits are commercially available that can stop the plague, if used properly. Remember to *read the label.*

Beer can also be used as a control. Pour the beer (stale or fresh; no special brand) into shallow containers, such as tuna or cat food cans, and place them about every six feet in the garden. The slugs crawl into the beer and seem to die quite happily. This procedure must be used early in the season, though, to gain control of the first brood. Otherwise, when they mature, they just crawl through the beer and go to work on your plants.

SQUASH VINE BORER
Who Pulled the Plug?

If you are standing in the middle of the cucurbit patch on a hot summer day, and the plants seem to wilt before your very eyes, it is probably not because you forgot to water them. The culprit could be the squash vine borer. This garden pest can become a major problem without your recognizing it until it is too late. The borer overwinters in the soil in the larva or pupa stage and emerges as a wasp-like moth in early summer to deposit its egg on the stem of the cucurbit plant, usually near the base. The egg hatches in about one week and the tiny larva tunnels into the stem. Once inside, it eats away the tissue that conducts water and nutrients to the upper parts of the plant. The damage may have a sawdust-like appearance, or show as a soft, mushy stem.

To control the squash vine borer, you may wish to use a pesticide cleared for this control, or you may wish to wait until later in the season to plant your crop. If you wait until midsummer to plant cucurbits, the adult borer will visit your garden early and find nothing on which to deposit its egg. Then, perhaps, it will go to your neighbor's.

If you find the borer has entered the plant (look for a tiny hole near the base of the stem), split the stem with a razor blade, locate the borer, and destroy it. Look for more than one borer while you are at it. After the operation, pile soil over the wounded area of the stem and keep it moist. There is a chance that the stem will take root and the plant will continue to grow and produce fruit. This won't work if the plant has already collapsed.

The squash vine borer will attack almost all of the cucurbit family, which include squash, cucumbers, melons, and pumpkins.

CUTWORMS IN THE VEGETABLE PATCH
Nothing Left

Planting tomatoes, eggplants, and peppers can be lots of fun and reward you with the fruit they produce. But there is a little "critter" which can spell disaster lurking in the soil. The morning after putting out your transplants can be quite a shock. If they have all been cut off at ground level don't blame the neighbor's kids. It probably wasn't rabbits, woodchucks, or deer either. The damage was most likely caused by the cutworm, a grub that lives its larval stage in the soil and eats at night. If you have had trouble with this pest in the past, you can almost be guaranteed you will have it again in the future.

To control the cutworm, collars can be placed around each transplant. Coated paper cups work well. Take the bottom out and slip the cup down over the plant. Press the lower part of the cup into the soil to a depth of at least one inch. This will provide a barrier the cutworm will not be able to penetrate.

General control of the cutworm starts with garden cleanup in the fall. Keep the garden weed-free and cultivate the soil to destroy the eggs laid by the adult moth. Sanitation goes a long way in controlling this and many other pests. Soil treatments with pesticides cleared for use in the vegetable patch are an alternative control. *Read the label and follow the manufacturer's recommended rates and directions.*

I have read that planting marigolds around tomatoes, eggplants, and peppers will repel the cutworm. The trouble with this is the cutworm can't read. The first night he eats the marigolds and the second night he eats the vegetables.

JAPANESE BEETLES
On the Attack

The Japanese beetle arrived in the United States in 1916 on nursery stock delivered to the East coast. Now it is a pest of commercial agriculture, as well as the home garden, in every state east of the Mississippi River, and has even been found on the West coast.

The Japanese beetle does double damage. The grub, which lives in the soil, attacks the roots of our trees, shrubs, lawns, vegetables, annuals, and perennials. The adults, both the male and the female, chew on the foliage or flowers, eating roses, lilacs, hydrangeas, viburnums, tomatoes, beans, and just about any other plant in our landscape.

To control the Japanese beetle there are several approaches that may be taken. They can be stopped in the grub stage by using the milky spore disease, which lives on and eventually kills the grub, or by the proper use of a pesticide as a soil treatment at the time the grubs are eating the roots off the plants.

The adults may be trapped. There are traps that have lures which attract the adults and then catch them in a receptacle that they cannot crawl out of. If you purchase a trap, be sure it contains attractants for the male and female, as you want to catch both. The trap should be placed to draw the beetles away from the area being protected. Pesticides for chewing insects can also be used to aid control. *Read the label.*

RACCOON
The Bandit

Sweet corn is not the easiest nor the most productive crop you can grow in the vegetable garden, because it takes up so much space and is attacked by the corn earworm and the European corn borer. These two pests can be controlled by the proper use of selected pesticides.

Throughout suburbia and rural America there is another little critter, not as easy to control, that can absolutely wipe out the corn patch in one night. He is the raccoon — that little animal who always looks as if he is going to a masquerade party, but the only party he is going to is the one in your corn patch. His celebration starts the night before you are ready to pick the first ears.

Here are two suggestions that may help to discourage Mr. Raccoon and keep him out of the patch.

Use two portable radios that you can set in the garden at night. Dial one radio to an all-night talk show and the other to a different station with talk. This provides confusing noise. Be sure to change the station on one radio each night so he doesn't get used to a particular voice. Do not play music or the raccoon will arrive, strip off the ears, and enjoy his corn to the sound of the latest hits. Start this procedure about one week before the corn is ready to eat.

The other control is to set up a low voltage electric fence. Circle the patch with one wire strand about five inches off the ground and another about fifteen inches off the ground. When the raccoon touches the wire, he will receive a slight shock. At this point he will tell the rest of his family "not to touch" and you will have won the battle.

"What's on the other side of the wall?"

WOODCHUCKS
Out of Sight, Out of Mind?

That harmless-looking little critter known as the woodchuck can devour the lettuce, cabbage, broccoli, and Brussels sprouts in virtually one night. He is not picky; he will eat the little seedlings or the mature plants. The vegetable garden is *not* safe if he is around. He is one of the most crafty critters there are. If you construct a fence, he will crawl over it, or tunnel under it, but there may be a way to keep him out. Line the inside of the fence with tar-paper or black plastic. If you eliminate his view of "lunch" he will not know it's there. "Out of sight, out of mind" — we hope.

Using a "live bait trap" is somewhat effective; however, you should check with your local ASPCA to review the regulations concerning how to trap him and where to release him. If you rent or buy such a trap, wash it and then let it sit out in the garden for a few days to eliminate the human scent. Put on a pair of rubber gloves and then wash your hands again. Using a head of cabbage for bait, peel off the outer leaves, again to remove the human scent, and put one half of the head in the trap and sprinkle the leaves from the other half along his trail. You may catch him, and you may not. Good luck.

MOLES
An Underground Railroad

There could be an underground railroad in your garden and lawn without your knowing it — that is, until there are piles of soil pushed up, or wiggly tunnels near the surface. The tunnels become quite pronounced in dry weather as the grasses die out above them. This is the visible sign of damage caused by the mole.

The mole is a blind rodent that lives in the soil and eats grubs, slugs, and other soil insects. Moles left unchecked cause great damage because they separate the plant roots from soil contact. This dries out the roots, resulting in the death of the plant.

Moles can be controlled with three basic methods. The elimination of the food stuffs (grubs) for the mole is probably the easiest. Grub-proof the growing area with a specially formulated pesticide and the moles will go somewhere else to eat.

Mole traps are terminal for the mole and his family. They are spring-loaded "pitchforks" that pierce the mole when the trap is released. Setting the trap early in the morning, on a fresh run, will result in one dead mole by noon. Continue trapping because there will be a whole family. Follow the directions that are supplied with the trap.

Vibration is another control. Miniature windmills that you see on a lawn are not there to generate energy or pump water. They are there to provide a "thumping" vibration in the soil. As the windmill rotates, a little foot at the base "thumps" the soil. This vibration will drive the mole elsewhere. (This does not work when there is no wind.)

WASPS AND HORNETS
At the Barbecue

Sitting on the patio or deck, sipping a large glass of iced tea on a hot day, can be an enjoyable experience. That is, until the wasps and hornets arrive. They will drive you indoors shortly, if they are not controlled. Wasps and hornets can attack unprovoked. Their stings can be very painful, and even deadly, if you are allergic.

Both pests can be controlled with a little persistence and caution. When you first observe them, watch the flight pattern and this will lead you to their home. Once you have discovered their nest, you can plan your attack. Obtain a pesticide specifically formulated to kill wasps and hornets. There are several brands available that will do the job. *Read the label.*

At sundown, put on a coat, a hat that you can pull down over your ears, gloves that can be tied around your sleeves, and go to work. (The reason for waiting until sundown is that this is the time they all return to the nest for a night's rest.) Your pesticide will kill them all if you spray the nest thoroughly. Some pressurized cans of spray shoot a straight 10-foot stream of pesticide. This will enable you to stand away from the nest and allow you to get a head start on the pest in case he should get excited and decide to head for you. If that happens — run!